Building Internationalized Spaces

Building Internationalized Spaces

Second Language Perspectives on Developing Language and Cultural Exchange Programs in Higher Education

EDITED BY **Matthew Allen**
Estela Ene
Kyle McIntosh

University of Michigan Press
Ann Arbor

Copyright © by the University of Michigan 2022
All rights reserved
Published in the United States of America
The University of Michigan Press
Printed and bound by CPI Group (UK) Ltd, Croydon, CR0 4YY

ISBN-13: 978-0-472-03883-1 (print)
ISBN-13: 978-0-472-22031-1 (ebook)

2025   2024   2023   2022   4   3   2   1

Acknowledgments

We would like to acknowledge the hard work and dedication of Kelly Sippell, Charles Watkinson, Scott Ham, Alan Bradshaw, Jennifer Simington, Danielle Coty-Fattal, and everyone else at University of Michigan Press who helped guide this book through the publication process. Their collective expertise, enthusiasm, and patience were vital to moving this project past the proposal stage, through several rounds of revision, and into print.

We express our deep gratitude to all of the authors who contributed to this volume. Without your individual chapters, this book would not have provided the varied and insightful perspectives needed to address such a complex topic. On behalf of everyone involved in this project, we would like to recognize our colleagues and students at our respective institutions who stand at the forefront of efforts to internationalize higher education.

Our sincere thanks go out to Christine Tardy and Gail Shuck for providing valuable feedback on early drafts of these chapters, as well as to our anonymous reviewers whose detailed comments helped us to strengthen the entire volume.

Lastly, we would like to thank our families for their love and support. We couldn't have done it without you!

Acknowledgment of Contribution

The editors' names appear in alphabetical order to indicate equal contribution.

Contents

List of Figures and Tables

About the Editors

Matthew Allen is the assistant director of curriculum and instruction at the Purdue Language and Cultural Exchange (PLaCE), an English for Academic Purposes program at Purdue University. He has led and participated in a variety of initiatives to develop internationalized programming at the university. His teaching and scholarly interests include second language reading and writing.

Estela Ene is an associate professor at Indiana University-Purdue University Indianapolis, where she directs the English for Academic Purposes program and the MA in TESOL program. She is involved in campus internationalization through faculty professional development and curriculum innovation. Her research interests include ESL/EFL writing, professional development, and online teaching.

Kyle McIntosh is an assistant professor of English and writing at the University of Tampa, where he teaches in the Academic Writing and TESOL certificate programs. His research interests include second language writing and assessment, intercultural rhetoric, and the politics of English language teaching.

About the Contributors

D. Hannah Bush is a lecturer at Purdue University, where she teaches in the Purdue Language and Cultural Exchange (PLaCE) program. Her interests include curriculum design and public health promotion and behavior among diverse populations.

Lixia Cheng is the assistant director of testing for the Purdue Language and Cultural Exchange (PLaCE). She worked extensively in the Oral English Proficiency Program (OEPP) during her PhD career as a graduate testing coordinator, research assistant, and graduate instructor.

Emmanuelle S. Chiocca is an assistant professor at Duke Kunshan University, where she co-directs the Third Space Lab. Her research lies at the intersection of transformative learning, language learning motivation, and intercultural communication in international higher education.

Mary Ann Cohen is a senior lecturer at Indiana University-Purdue University Indianapolis (IUPUI) who teaches professional writing skills, business and administrative writing, and first-year composition courses to English as a first language and multilingual writers.

Kathleen A. Corrales is an assistant professor at the Universidad del Norte. Her research interests include language teaching and learning, CLIL, global business communication, internationalization, and intercultural competence.

Joseph A. Davies is senior lecturer of English language at Duke Kunshan University. He is a senior fellow of the Higher Education Academy and researches higher education feedback literacy, EAP instruction and pedagogy, and language classroom assessment.

Laura J. Davies is senior lecturer of English language and assistant director of EAP at Duke Kunshan University. She is a senior fellow of the Higher Education Academy and her research interests include intercultural engagement and course design.

Nancy Farner is a lecturer with the Purdue Language and Cultural Exchange (PLaCE), where she helps international students develop academic, linguistic, and cultural competencies. Her professional interests include curriculum development and design, language learning, and intercultural competency.

Ghada Gherwash is the director of the Farnham Writers' Center and an assistant professor of writing at Colby College. Her research interests include second language writing, writing center theory and L2 writers, intercultural communication, and language planning.

Kristin E. Hiller is an assistant professor and the associate director of the Language and Culture Center at Duke Kunshan University, where she directs the Writing and Language Studio and teaches academic writing. She researches language policy and writing pedagogy in transnational higher education contexts.

Cristine McMartin-Miller is a teaching professor at Northeastern University, where she teaches and oversees courses for international students and is the program coordinator of the International Tutoring Center.

Lucie Moussu is an associate professor and director of the Writing Centre at the Royal Military College in Kingston, Ontario. Her research interests include writing center administration and second language writing.

Saghar L. Naghib is a senior lecturer of English language at Duke Kunshan University and co-directs the Third Space Lab. She is also a conflict resolution practitioner and researches aggravated conflicts among fragile communities.

Lourdes Rey Paba is an associate professor at Universidad del Norte. Her research interests include classroom assessment, curriculum design, teacher development, language learning, and internationalization of higher education.

Nadezda Pimenova is a lecturer at Purdue University, where she teaches in the Purdue Language and Cultural Exchange (PLaCE) program. Currently, she is interested in second language acquisition and humor comprehension.

Rodrigo A. Rodríguez-Fuentes is an assistant professor at Universidad del Norte in Colombia. His research interests include assessment and testing procedures applied to EFL, language pedagogy, and interculturality.

Nayibe Rosado-Mendinueta is a language teacher and teacher educator at Universidad del Norte in Colombia. Her research includes students and teacher learning in contexts such as classrooms and other institutions.

Tanita Saenkhum is an associate professor at the University of Tennessee, Knoxville, where she specializes in second language writing with a focus on placement, assessment, and writing teacher education.

Silvia Sgaramella is a doctoral candidate in modern languages and a writing center tutor at the University of Alberta. Her research includes writing studies, technical communication, and second language acquisition.

Hannah Soblo is a PhD candidate of rhetoric, writing, and linguistics at the University of Tennessee, Knoxville. Her research interests include sociolinguistics, second language writing, and writing program administration.

Kevin M. Sprague is a lecturer in the Language and Culture Center at Duke Kunshan University, where he teaches academic writing and communication skills. He also focuses on teacher development and facilitates teacher training throughout China.

Xin Zhang is an assistant professor at Duke Kunshan University, where she directs the Chinese as a Second Language Program and co-directs the Third Space Lab. Her research interests lie at the intersection of applied linguistics, Chinese language pedagogy, and intercultural communication.

Introduction:
L2 Expertise in Curriculum Internationalization

Matthew Allen, Estela Ene, and Kyle McIntosh

Internationalization has been a driving force in higher education for several decades now. It is an enormously complex phenomenon, requiring stakeholders to balance financial imperatives with educational outcomes in dynamic geopolitical, economic, and sociocultural environments. Many colleges and universities around the world continue to pursue internationalization in terms of student populations, research programs, and institutional partnerships, but frequently the curriculum and instruction remain rooted in a unidirectional model that aims primarily to help international students adapt to the existing norms and expectations of the local community. Too often, linguistic and cultural differences among students continue to be seen as problems to be solved rather than resources that can contribute to what should be the goals of internationalization: improved communication, better understanding, and more meaningful exchanges among people of diverse backgrounds. As Jones and Killick (2007) pointed out, "responding to the diversity of international students and responding to the diversity of home students are in fact not two agendas but one" (p. 110). This comprehensive view demands that more attention be given to cultivating the *international/ global* in all students while supporting the specific needs of unique student populations and learning contexts.

As colleges and universities recognize the importance of these goals and the ethical obligations to support international students as a distinct population, they are faced with an important logistical challenge: how to build more globally aware programs and pedagogies into the

1

local campus to make transformative practices and outcomes available to everyone. This book provides case studies from higher educational contexts to represent the diverse ways that second language (L2) specialists can build programs and courses that contribute to their institutions' internationalization by promoting language and cultural exchange. We present examples of internationalization through the curriculum and co-curriculum in a variety of countries to highlight ways in which L2 specialists and programs have advanced internationalization by diversifying support for international students and creating engagement between international and local students, for the benefit of both.

Internationalization of Higher Education

Internationalization of higher education (IoHE), in de Wit and Hunter's (2015) revision of Knight's (2003) definition, is "the *intentional* process of integrating an international, intercultural or global dimension into the purpose, functions and delivery of post-secondary education, *in order to enhance the quality of education and research for all students and staff, and to make a meaningful contribution to society*" (p. 3, italics in original). Although one motivation is the promise of increased tuition dollars and other forms of revenue, IoHE has substantive merits for participants; notably, it facilitates more diverse exchanges of knowledge among researchers and better prepares students to live and work in the global environments of the 21st century (Hudzik, 2011).

IoHE has been occurring in the larger context of increased mobility created by a globalized economy that, over the last 30 years, has led many people to pursue international higher education as a way to gain access to better opportunities at home and abroad. According to the Open Doors report compiled by the Institute of International Education (2020), more than 340,000 U.S. university students studied abroad as part of their degree programs in 2017–2018 (with most studying for less than an academic or calendar year). Additionally, many students from other countries come to the United States or go to other host countries for short- or mid-term study abroad or to pursue degrees as international undergraduate and graduate students. Although international student enrollment at U.S. universities has slowed in terms of annual percentage growth since the 2015–2016 academic year, 1,095,299 international students came to the United States during the 2018–2019 academic year (Institute of International Education, 2020). Similarly, in 2017, 1.7 million students from abroad studied at universities across the 28 states of the European Union (Eurostat, 2019). Although during the COVID-19 pandemic student mobility decreased dramatically, experts believe it will remain an essential component of IoHE, as there is no substitute for the first-hand experience one gains through travel (de Wit & Jones, 2021). Other means of achieving IoHE present more accessible alternatives, such as virtual exchanges and internationalization-at-home strategies.

Internationalization Abroad and at Home

IoHE is a complex phenomenon that comprises two main areas: internationalization *abroad* and internationalization *at home*. **Internationalization abroad** entails student mobility, academic credit, and degree mobility (such as dual/transfer credit between international institutions and dual degree programs), as well as staff and faculty mobility (e.g., international hiring, visiting scholars). **Internationalization at home (IaH)** refers to the internationalization of campuses not only through the recruitment of international students but also through the internationalization of the curriculum and co-curricular activities. Simply put, internationalization abroad relies mainly on sending a relatively small number of students or faculty to foreign destinations, while internationalization at home refers to efforts to bring international experiences and global perspectives to all students and faculty at a college or university as part of their "normal" campus activities (Nilsson, 2003).

Both ways of pursuing internationalization have merit and can lead to transformative, measurable learning outcomes (Deardorff, 2015). In particular, both types of internationalization can improve the intercultural competence of those involved. Deardorff (2006) defined intercultural competence as the "ability to communicate effectively and appropriately in intercultural situations based on one's intercultural knowledge, skills, and attitudes" (p. 241). Deardorff (2015) expanded that earlier definition into a model whose essential elements include knowledge (of one's own and others' perspectives), skills (ranging from observing and listening to adapting one's thinking and behavior to other cultures), and attitudes (of openness, curiosity, and respect toward other perspectives).

Within IaH, *curriculum internationalization* stands out as a means to disseminate the goals of internationalization—increased intercultural knowledge and sensitivity, an understanding of the relationships between the local and the global, and positive attitudes of respect and curiosity toward other cultures—throughout any and all subjects taught. Since learning happens in ungraded activities outside the classroom, at academic support services, and in informal interactions, it follows that the co-curriculum needs to be as internationalized as the curriculum (Leask, 2015). Furthermore, it is evident that for internationalization to work to everyone's benefit, it needs to be comprehensive: preparation for it and participation in it has to include all faculty, staff, students, curriculum, services, etc. (Hudzik, 2011). Finally, comprehensive internationalization requires interculturalization (Jones, 2019); if the actors involved in campus life become more interculturally involved and competent, the deeper goals of internationalization can be accomplished. This volume provides examples of curricular and co-curricular designs in which L2 specialists and programs advance those deeper goals.

Increasingly, scholars and institutions recognize that the relatively few students who have the opportunity to study abroad are not the only ones who can benefit from participating in meaningful international educational experiences (Landorf, Doscher, & Hardrick, 2018). Academic and local communities stand to gain far more than revenue from the participation of international students (Castro et al., 2016; Charles & Deardorff, 2014). Their peers and teachers, as well as others in the communities where these international students live, work, or volunteer, also benefit by developing more global mindsets and intercultural competence (Jones, 2013). While not always tied to linguistic outcomes, IaH itself is defined as "the purposeful integration of international and *intercultural dimensions* into the formal and informal curriculum for all students within domestic learning environments" (Beelen & Jones, 2015, p. 69; emphasis added).

The Goals and Challenges of Internationalization Abroad and at Home

The intentional, purposeful pursuit of international and intercultural dimensions is a crucial aspect of IaH, and one that counters certain myths about internationalization. For example, conventional wisdom has long held that students who depart their home for educational experiences abroad will be immersed in rich language and cultural learning environments and that such immersion will automatically lead to transformative international experiences. Unfortunately, recent scholarship has shown this assumption to be more myth than reality (Castro et al., 2016; Vande Berg, Paige, & Lou, 2012). This "immersion myth" ignores the complexities and difficulties that many students face in terms of their linguistic and intercultural development (DeKeyser, 2007; Hammer, 2012). It also tends to exaggerate the role of study abroad in campus internationalization (Charles & Deardorff, 2014). Even at universities with large numbers of international students, IoHE initiatives often do not sufficiently consider the contributions of their diverse student population. Philosophically, such oversights may arise from viewing international students from a deficit perspective, which holds that successful academic and research activity can only begin once this population has been linguistically and culturally "remedied" (see Benzie, 2010; Siczek & Shapiro, 2014). When institutions do not commit to the academic, social, and personal needs of international students, there is a greater potential for their exclusion or exploitation (Sherry, Thomas, & Chui, 2010). Clearly, the mere presence of international students on a campus cannot guarantee internationalization outcomes at home.

An ongoing and important challenge is figuring out how to incorporate international perspectives into established disciplinary programs, courses, and instruction (Castro et al., 2016). Curriculum internationalization involves the integration of global perspectives and learning goals into course design and instruction, but it presupposes that campus administration will ensure the necessary professional development of the faculty involved. Capacity also needs to be built for extra- and co-curricular activities that are geared toward internationalization. Educational reform at this level is no easy endeavor, but it is a worthy, even necessary one (Hudzik, 2011), as the true goal of internationalization is to benefit all those involved (Charles & Deardorff, 2014; Hudzik, 2011).

Finally, the development of not only second language (L2) proficiency but also intercultural competency for all are at a high premium in IaH. L2 proficiency and intercultural competency develop from a complex, dynamic set of interactions among students, their educational environments, and the educators who support them. There are many ways for students to develop L2 proficiency and intercultural competence, but these opportunities require intentional, research-inspired contributions from L2 learning specialists, applied linguists, content-area faculty, and the host-country community (Jackson, 2018). For students to develop the skills, knowledge, and attitudes that are the desired outcomes of internationalization, they need training and support before, during, and after their international educational experiences (e.g., Engle & Engle, 2012; Galante, 2014).

IaH implies that any program or field can, to a certain extent, target the development of intercultural competence. As Vande Berg, Paige, and Lou (2012) emphasized, all learning experiences are situated in specific cultural and linguistic contexts. In their work on learning in study abroad, they have made the point that students will get much more out of their trips abroad if they are prepared appropriately by educators. By the same token, educators teaching in their home departments should consider how their own praxis is culturally bound and how they can more effectively engage with diverse student populations. Resources that educators can use as catalysts to revise or expand their praxis include the AAC&U (2009) VALUE rubric for Intercultural Knowledge and Competence, the AAC&U (2014) VALUE rubric for Global Learning, Jane Jackson's (2014) textbook *Introducing Language and Intercultural Communication*, and Kate Berardo and Darla Deardorff's (2012) edited volume, which provides research-based frameworks and learning activities for trainers and educators who need to prepare students to have meaningful intercultural encounters.

As we will argue, it is important to recognize that L2 specialists and programs are vital resources for training other faculty, collaborating across academic units, and spearheading co-curricular activities. By virtue of their expertise, L2 specialists and programs are already organically implementing internationalization for the benefit of faculty and students at home.

The Role of Second Language Specialists and Programs in IoHE/IaH

The importance of intercultural and linguistic competence in internationalization signals the crucial role of language and culture professionals and programs in IoHE efforts. As L2 specialists working with international students on our respective campuses, we have been considering these questions independently and now together:

1. How do international students bring diversity to our campuses?
2. How can international diversity be more widely shared with domestic students?
3. How do we bring international students to experience diversity on our campuses?

Given the global push for IoHE, we know that many colleagues around the world are pondering similar questions in their own educational contexts. This volume, therefore, takes a step toward finding answers by presenting case studies that illustrate how L2 faculty, administrators, and programs have contributed to IoHE on their campuses in impactful ways.

The impetus for this volume is our own experiences as L2 specialists engaged in English as a Second Language (ESL) program administration and instruction on our respective campuses, where we have witnessed the opportunities and challenges of IoHE in various ways. At the student level, we have witnessed both positive and negative instances of diverse students figuring out how to work together or build friendships. We have also talked extensively with colleagues and faculty from other disciplines about the challenges of fostering engagement among diverse students for mutual benefits and about accounting for linguistic and cultural differences. Given such realities, we have worked on our campuses to explore practical approaches to the ways that language and cultural differences among students can become opportunities to enrich and enhance the quality of post-secondary education for all students and faculty, rather than barriers to communication and understanding.

Based on our experiences and observations of trends in higher education, we know that L2 specialists and programs contribute to and benefit from conversations about how to further IaH efforts. L2 specialists are inherently sensitive to many aspects of internationalization, especially in relation to student-facing efforts (e.g., designing pedagogical applications that target intercultural competence and language learning and/ or understanding students' experiences preparing for and studying in international contexts). L2 specialists also tend to be teachers who know how to teach multicultural student populations and approach cultural difference and diversity. Many are teacher trainers who know what other teachers need to know to successfully engage international and domestic students. They include program administrators who understand their diverse student populations in the larger campus and social context.

We readily acknowledge that this expertise is not exclusive to those who have a background in applied linguistics/TESOL/second language studies or roles in ESL/English for Academic Purposes (EAP) programs, but this volume recognizes the work of L2 specialists with such backgrounds first and foremost because this is our community of practice. However, collaborations with specialists from related fields and programs (writing/rhetoric and composition, for example) are featured. Thus, this collection is an effort to contribute to unified discussions: (1) among L2 specialists, who tend to see themselves or frame their work in terms of their specialty or type of program (e.g., EAP, reading, international teaching assistant (ITA) support); (2) among those in higher education who tend to orient toward their disciplinary values, conventions, and practices; and (3) among L2 specialists and other educators who may find it challenging to make meaningful curricular changes to incorporate international diversity. Ultimately, comprehensive internationalization means that everyone at the institution needs to be involved by finding common ground while still maintaining their distinct academic identities and ways of knowing. We believe that the bigger tent of IoHE provides room for L2 specialists in specific departments (e.g., English or world languages) to find common ground with fields that share many common interests (such as intercultural communication or study abroad).

Although scholars have pointed out that internationalization "should no longer be considered in terms of a westernized, largely Anglo-Saxon, and predominantly English-speaking paradigm" (Jones & de Wit, 2014, p. 28), in many contexts, internationalization continues to be tied to learning English (Weiser & Rose, 2018). The influx of international students to universities in English-dominant countries solidifies the need to learn English before and during the students' stay, strengthening the status of English as a global lingua franca. At the same time, to remain competitive, higher education institutions around the world have had to internationalize (de Wit & Hunter, 2015), in many cases offering English-medium instruction to attract international students, which further highlights the need for English proficiency and intercultural competence. Both situations illuminate the centrality of English language—and those who specialize in teaching it—to internationalization initiatives. However, few nods have been given in internationalization studies to the crucial role that English language professionals and programs play in internationalization initiatives. Likewise, within their home fields, language and culture scholars and practitioners have failed to label their own work as significant to internationalization, perhaps seeing much of it as "business as usual."

This Collection in Context

Building Internationalized Spaces aims to bring to the forefront the contributions of those working in various language-related fields within higher education that go beyond "just teaching English" and toward preparing the global citizens of the future. We see this volume as contributing to emerging interdisciplinary conversations in higher education about how to refine internationalization in terms of praxis and how to coordinate curricular and pedagogical efforts to achieve meaningful learning outcomes for all students. The work presented in this volume is relevant to several areas in higher education research and practice that share interests and values in regard to student learning and internationalization, including intercultural communication, writing studies, study abroad, virtual exchange, and academic support. Because of disciplinary and administrative boundaries, such works may not otherwise be presented side by side. Thus, we hope that our volume fosters further conversation across these boundaries in higher education.

A few recent contributions by scholars in such fields as applied linguistics, TESOL, and writing studies have made an explicit connection between professionals in these areas and internationalization. For example, Rose and Weiser (2018) noted in their edited volume of perspectives of various writing program administrators that "thinking about a changing student population has led them to recognize that revised administrative structures, curricular revisions, and new professional-development programs improve teaching and learning not just for international students but for all students" (p. 7). While offering clear guidance for internationalizing the writing curriculum, Lape (2020) contends in only an implicit way with aspects of teaching English to international students in the context of writing courses. Siczek and Shapiro (2014) present TESOL/EAP-Writing Across the Curriculum (WAC) collaborations as a way to promote not only internationalization and global learning for all but also diversity, equity, and inclusion goals. Bond (2020) argues that language learning is vital to internationalization efforts and must be foregrounded across the curriculum. She then suggests several promising strategies for doing so (e.g., connecting academic and social support), but the book focuses mainly on a single institutional context and the disconnect that exists there between those who specialize in EAP and their colleagues in other disciplines.

While we agree that more needs to be done to bridge such gaps, we also feel that it is important to recognize successful attempts at integrating English language–learning international students into the campus through the curriculum or co-curriculum and to shine light on positive examples of leveraging the expertise of teachers, researchers, and administrators who work with these students. Such is the motivation for our work on our respective campuses and the work presented in this volume. Because the realization of IaH values and goals is still emerging, much work lies ahead for curriculum and program development as well as in research to measure the effects and effectiveness on student learning. This volume serves a bridging role to connect the broad set of values related to internationalization, on the one hand, to students using a second language to study in international contexts or global programs.

Overview of Chapters

The chapters included in this volume identify specific, innovative ways to work on the outcomes of IoHE/IaH from the perspectives of L2 specialists, program administrators, and instructors. We encouraged the authors to take a grounded approach to writing about internationalization efforts where they live. Framing it within the work they do on their respective campuses, the authors in this volume examine institutional internationalization through the lenses of language learning and intercultural engagement. Each chapter offers a distinct perspective on L2 learning and the intercultural development of adult learners in different academic settings. The authors provide suggestions for how L2 specialists can reframe their work in their individual programs to help internationalize the entire university in ways that lead to improved learning outcomes for students at different points in their degree programs, such as:

- ○ orientation programs (early arrival on campus, before classes start)
- ○ language center contexts (support during studies)
- ○ volunteer programs for ITAs and undergraduate students
- ○ graduate-level writing support structures

○ instructional design (virtual learning spaces)

○ co-curricular virtual partner programs

○ intercultural composition (i.e., promoting intentional placement, interdisciplinary collaborations)

By focusing on the question of how to best support and integrate multilingual international students at the undergraduate and graduate levels, both inside and outside of academic courses, this collection offers options and approaches that have been developed to fit the needs and circumstances of a specific context but that could be adapted for other contexts.

This collection is intentionally international in its focus. We invited authors from both outside and inside the United States to participate, targeting spaces in the curriculum and on campus where language and cultural exchange efforts could be highlighted and developed further (see Leask, 2015). The chapters in Part I detail efforts at four universities around the world to revise the curriculum in innovative ways that resist the deficit model of language learning and cultural knowledge by providing academic support for international students beyond so-called remedial classes and working to foster greater collaboration with their domestic peers. In Chapter 1, Chiocca, Davies, Davies, Hiller, Naghib, Sprague, and Zhang address the immersion myth head-on by stressing the need for explicit instruction in language and intercultural awareness from the moment students arrive on campus. The authors provide an overview of the four-day student orientation program at Duke Kunshan University (DKU), during which students work on collaborative, community-based, bilingual (Chinese and English) activities and discussions. Preliminary survey findings indicate high levels of satisfaction and preparedness among all participating students.

Even with innovative orientation programs in place, students continue to need language and culture support throughout their studies. Often, this comes in the form of a one- or two-semester ESL course that may or may not count toward graduation. After completing such a course, international and domestic multilingual students may find themselves taking other courses that pay little attention to their specific needs or unique perspectives. In Chapter 2, McMartin-Miller addresses this shortcoming in her chronicle of the development of the International Tutoring Center (ITC) at Northeastern University, which offers individual, group, and online tutorials that address a range of skills and needs for multilingual students, from career preparation to casual conversation. This case study shows the importance of having a designated unit on campus that can provide ongoing, multifaceted language and culture support.

Advancements in digital technologies present a range of possibilities for offering such support beyond traditional classroom settings. In Chapter 3, Bush, Allen, Farner, and Pimenova present an innovative approach to designing virtual learning spaces within an undergraduate EAP course at Purdue University that has helped students work toward IaH outcomes while meeting the course objectives. The authors show how the use of video blogs and digital storytelling invites students to express and develop their intercultural identities in ways that not only "change our students' understanding of themselves and others, but [also show] that they can change others' preconceived notions and expectations about what it means to be an international student" (p. TBD).

The final two chapters in Part I describe partner programs that are embedded in English-language courses at two universities. In Chapter 4, Rodríguez-Fuentes, Corrales, Paba, and Rosado-Mendinueta discuss the implementation of virtual exchanges (VEs) between students at Universidad del Norte in Colombia and Spanish student partners at a U.S. university that allow for IaH to occur in a higher education setting that has few international students. These web-based pen pals create authentic opportunities for students to practice the language skills they have learned in class and to improve their intercultural competence. VEs also appear to be well-suited for situations like a global pandemic where students are unable to travel abroad and must take classes online. In Chapter 5, Cheng provides the historical institutional context for internationalization efforts at Purdue University to show how a program that connects undergraduate domestic students with ITAs is meaningful for this context and beneficial for both student populations;

the ITA partner program facilitates the sociocultural integration of international students into the university while equipping domestic students with international skills and knowledge.

The chapters included in Part II explore issues of L2 writing and cross-cultural composition in undergraduate and graduate programs at institutions large and small. Since most colleges and universities in North America require all students to take introductory composition classes, writing programs are an important site for addressing both the theoretical and practical issues of IaH through their work on language use and knowledge sharing. The section moves from general to specific, beginning with an administrative perspective on cross-cultural composition and then moving to implementations in writing classrooms and writing centers. In Chapter 6, Saenkhum and Soblo provide an overview of the assessment and placement options that the composition program at the University of Tennessee (Knoxville) has considered in response to the rapid internationalization of its undergraduate population. The authors explain why and how program administrators implemented cross-cultural composition as a means of promoting interaction among L1 and L2 English-speaking students and of providing opportunities for all students to develop their intercultural communication skills through participation and collaboration in a multicultural, multilingual classroom environment.

In Chapter 7, Ene and Cohen present the case of a multicultural composition course at Indiana University–Purdue University Indianapolis (IUPUI) that aligns with the campus' strategic goal of internationalizing its student body, curriculum, and co-curriculum by serving both L1 and L2 speakers of English. In addition to presenting survey and reflection-based data, the authors describe how the syllabus and materials evolved over the course of three semesters. Similarly, in Chapter 8, Gherwash explains how internationalization efforts at Colby College, a small liberal arts college in the United States, have been implemented in the cross-cultural design of a first-year composition course. After describing the structure and content of the course, the author addresses the particular challenges of internationalization at smaller colleges, where faculty expertise and institutional resources can be much more limited than at large universities.

In Chapter 9, Moussu and Sgaramella introduce a non-traditional model to support L2 graduate students called the Guided Writing Instruction Group (GWIG), which aims to facilitate the learning of academic writing conventions among L2 graduate students and to respond to their frequent requests for help, along with requests from their supervisors and departments. Additionally, GWIGs help to boost students' self-confidence and improve their communicative skills so that they can become active members of their chosen discourse communities. Taken together, the chapters in Part II provide educators and administrators with innovative ways to use internationalization as a lens to revitalize existing composition classes and programs or to create new ones. Given the importance of writing in the academy, we further believe that this multifaceted consideration of writing spaces can help to make inroads into thinking about how to internationalize other areas of the curriculum.

We hope that language educators and program administrators who read this volume will benefit from seeing their own work framed within these discussions of IoHE and IaH while encountering new perspectives and insights about the local work involved in such efforts. We also hope that this volume will appeal to other stakeholders—particularly faculty, staff, and administrators who work with international student populations—and that they too will benefit by gaining a better understanding of how language and cultural issues are—sometimes unexpectedly—a vital aspect of internationalization efforts on any campus.

References

Association of American Colleges and Universities (AAC&U). (2009). *Intercultural knowledge and effectiveness VALUE rubric*. Retrieved from https://www.aacu.org/value/rubrics/intercultural-knowledge

Association of American Colleges and Universities (AAC&U). (2014). *Global learning VALUE rubric*. Retrieved from https://www.aacu.org/value/rubrics/global-learning

Berardo, K., & Deardorff, D. K. (2012). *Building cultural competence: Innovative activities and models*. Sterling, VA: Stylus.

Beelen, J., & Jones, E. (2015). Redefining internationalization at home. In A. Curaj, L. Matei, R. Pricopie, J. Salmi, & P. Scott (Eds.), *The European higher education area:*

Between critical reflections and future policies (pp. 59–72). Dordrecht, Netherlands: SpringerOpen. https://doi.org/10.1007/978-3-319-20877-0_5

Benzie, H. J. (2010). Graduating as a 'native speaker': International students and English language proficiency in higher education. *Higher Education Research & Development, 29*(4), 447–459. https://doi.org/10.1080/07294361003598824

Bond, B. (2020). *Making language visible in the university: English for academic purposes and internationalisation.* Bristol, England: Multilingual Matters.

Castro, P., Woodin, J., Lundgren, U., & Byram, M. (2016). Student mobility and internationalisation in higher education: Perspectives from practitioners. *Language and Intercultural Communication, 16*(3), 418–436. https://doi.org/10.1080/14708477.2016.1168052

Charles, H., & Deardorff, D. K. (2014, June 18). A failure to capitalize on globalization [WorldWise]. *The Chronicle of Higher Education.* Retrieved from http://www.chronicle.com/blogs/worldwise/a-failure-to-capitalize-on-globalization/339

Deardorff, D. K. (2006). Identification and assessment of intercultural competence as a student outcome of internationalization. *Journal of Studies in International Education, 10*(3), 241–266. https://doi.org/10.1177/1028315306287002

Deardorff, D. K. (2015). *Demystifying outcomes assessment for international educators: A practical approach.* Sterling, VA: Stylus.

DeKeyser, R. M. (2007). Study abroad as foreign language practice. In R. M. DeKeyser (Ed.), *Practice in a second language: Perspectives from applied linguistics and cognitive psychology* (pp. 208–226). Cambridge, England: Cambridge University Press.

de Wit, H., & Hunter, F. (2015). The future of internationalization of higher education in Europe. *International Higher Education, 83,* 2–3. https://doi.org/10.6017/ihe.2015.83.9073

de Wit, H., & Jones, E. (2021, June 9). *Internationalization as a global field.* Retrieved from https://www.youtube.com/watch?v=VQwahHy7GyM

Engle, L., & Engle, J. (2012). Beyond immersion: The American University Center of Provence experiment in holistic intervention. In M. Vande Berg, R. M. Paige, & K. H. Lou (Eds.), *Student learning abroad: What our students are learning, what they're not, and what we can do about it* (pp. 284–307). Sterling, VA: Stylus.

Eurostat. (2019). *Education and training in the EU: Facts and figures.* Retrieved from https://ec.europa.eu/eurostat/statistics-explained/index.php?title=Education_and_training_in_the_EU_-_facts_and_figures

Galante, A. (2014). Developing EAL learners' intercultural sensitivity through a digital literacy project. *TESL Canada Journal, 32*(1), 53. https://doi.org/10.18806/tesl.v32i1.1199

Hammer, M. R. (2012). The intercultural development inventory: A new frontier in assessment and development of intercultural competence. In M. Vande Berg, R. M. Paige, & K. H. Lou (Eds.), *Student Learning Abroad* (Vol. 5, pp. 115–136). Sterling, VA: Stylus.

Hudzik, J. K. (2011). *Comprehensive internationalization.* Washington, DC: NAFSA.

Institute of International Education (2020). Enrollment Trends. *Open Doors.* Retrieved from https://opendoorsdata.org/data/international-students/enrollment-trends/

Jackson, J. (2014). *Introducing language and intercultural communication.* London: Routledge.

Jackson, J. (2018). Intervening in the intercultural learning of L2 study abroad students: From research to practice. *Language Teaching, 51*(3), 365–382. https://doi.org/10.1017/S0261444816000392

Jones, E. (2013) Internationalization and employability: The role of intercultural experiences in the development of transferable skills. *Public Money and Management, 33*(2), 95–104.

Jones, E. (2019). Is it time to pursue "interculturalisation"? *Times Higher Education* September 26, 2019. https://timeshighereducation.com/opinion/it-time-pursue-interculturalization

Jones, E., & de Wit, H. (Spring 2014). "Globalized internationalization: Implications for policy and practice." IIEnetworker (pp. 28–29).

Jones, E., & Killick, D. (2007). Internationalization of the curriculum. In Jones, E., & Brown, S. (Eds.), *Internationalizing higher education* (pp. 109–119). London: Routledge.

Knight, J. (2003). Updated internationalization definition. *International Higher Education, 33*, 2–3.

Landorf, H., Doscher, S., & Hardrick, J. (2018). *Making global learning universal: Promoting inclusion and success for all students.* Sterling, VA: Stylus.

Lape, N. G. (2020). *Internationalizing the writing center: A guide for developing a multilingual writing center.* Anderson, SC: Parlor Press.

Leask, B. (2015). *Internationalizing the curriculum.* New York: Routledge.

Nilsson, B. (2003). Internationalisation at home from a Swedish perspective: The case of Malmö. *Journal of Studies in International Education, 7*(1), 27–40. doi:10.1177/1028315302250178

Sherry, M., Thomas, P., & Chui, W. H. (2010). International students: A vulnerable student population. *Higher Education, 60*(1), 33–46.

Siczek, M., & Shapiro, S. (2014). Developing writing-intensive courses for a globalized curriculum through WAC-TESOL collaborations. In T. M. Zawacki & M. Cox (Eds.),

WAC and second language writers: Research towards linguistically and culturally inclusive programs and practices (pp. 329–346). Fort Collins, CO: The WAC Clearinghouse and Parlor Press.

Vande Berg, M., Paige, R. M., & Lou, K. H. (2012). *Student learning abroad: What our students are learning, what they're not, and what we can do about it.* Sterling, VA: Stylus.

Weiser, I., & Rose, S. K. (2018). Internationalized writing programs in the twenty-first-century United States: Implications and opportunities. In S. K. Rose & I. Weiser (Eds.), *The internationalization of U.S. writing programs* (pp. 1–10). Logan: Utah State University Press.

Part I

Revising the Curriculum

1

Rethinking Orientation: Innovation and Collaboration in a Language and Culture Camp at a Sino–U.S. University

Emmanuelle S. Chiocca, Joseph A. Davies,
Laura J. Davies, Kristin E. Hiller, Saghar L.
Naghib, Kevin M. Sprague, and Xin Zhang

The past few decades have seen a dramatic increase in the internationalization of higher education institutions, from study abroad programs to increasing internationalization efforts at home (Institute of International Education, 2019; Ogden & Brewer, 2019). Many internationalized higher education institutions aim to develop intercultural competence and L2 proficiency, particularly in study abroad programs. Both are often assumed to be natural outcomes for students in these contexts. However, research suggests that simply spending time in another country, studying at an institution with a diverse student body, or even experiencing intercultural encounters are insufficient (Gurin, Day, Hurtado, & Gurin, 2002; Otten, 2003). Most students require explicit instruction and mentorship to develop these valued competencies (Brewer & Moore, 2015; Jackson, 2017, 2018a; Paige & Vande Berg, 2012). This chapter reports on an intervention during first-year student orientation at Duke Kunshan University (DKU), a newly established Sino–U.S. university in China. The primary goal of this orientation was to employ group activities that would foster connections among all incoming students, while delivering targeted instruction in language learning and academic skills.

Context

DKU is a Sino–U.S. joint venture university located in Jiangsu Province, China. English is its medium of instruction. The university began offering master's programs in 2014 and launched its interdisciplinary liberal arts and sciences undergraduate degree program in 2018. The undergraduate program includes a language requirement that students fulfill by taking either English for Academic Purposes (EAP) or Chinese as a Second Language (CSL). The first two undergraduate cohorts numbered approximately 255 and 320 students, roughly 30 percent of whom comprised international students from more than 30 countries. Slightly more than 50 percent of the international students are from North America (nearly all from the United States), while approximately 25 percent are from Asia, with South Korea and Pakistan accounting for half of the Asian international students. The remaining 25 percent are from Africa, Europe, Oceania, and South America (in descending order).

As a joint venture institution, DKU differs from the classic model of international universities (Knight, 2015) in some important ways. In the classic model, there is a host country population that is largely familiar with both the academic and wider cultural context of the institution and an international student body that is largely unfamiliar with these contexts and has varying levels of proficiency in the language of instruction. By contrast, at DKU, the international student body tends to have greater comfort with the language of instruction but still must adjust to a new institutional and broader cultural context, whereas the host country population must adapt to both a new academic and institutional culture *and* English-medium instruction. Thus, it can be argued that all incoming DKU students need to adapt to a new transnational higher education context (Caruana & Montgomery, 2015).

Given this shared need, most of the overall student orientation programming at DKU has been designed for all incoming students; there is no stand-alone orientation for international students (with the exception of sessions related to visas and other logistical matters). However, in the 2018 orientation, students were often segregated according to their language course track. International students spent much of their time in cultural and Chinese language orientation, while EAP-track students (all from greater China) participated in academic English workshops. As a result, there were fewer opportunities for integration among the two groups.

Throughout the first year of the undergraduate program, concerns were raised by faculty, administrators, and students about a perceived lack of integration and engagement among linguistically and culturally diverse groups of students. While not unique to DKU (e.g., Otten, 2003), the division of students into EAP and CSL groups during orientation may have inadvertently contributed to this behavior. As they were adjusting to the culturally diverse environment, many students were additionally challenged by the academic and linguistic demands of DKU. To address these challenges, the Language and Culture Center (LCC) designed and implemented a new four-day camp-like program during first-year orientation in August 2019 called "Language and Culture Days." This was an intentional intervention, aimed at bringing all incoming students together through activities that foster interaction and learning within diverse student groups.

Literature Review

In a context of growing suspicion regarding the effects of international sojourns, researcher-practitioners have challenged the "immersion myth" that simply being in an environment with multiple cultures and languages leads to higher L2 proficiency and intercultural competence (Halenko et al., 2019; Jackson, 2015; Kinginger, 2009; Paige & Vande Berg, 2012). By *intercultural competence*, we mean "the ability to communicate effectively and appropriately in intercultural situations based on one's intercultural knowledge, skills, and attitudes" (Deardorff, 2006, pp. 247–248). Some interculturalists additionally observe that students frequently remain in cultural and linguistic silos, occasionally leading to feelings of cultural antagonism or superiority (Block, 2007; Terzuolo, 2018).

There is now broad agreement that students benefit from *interventions* (Jackson, 2017, 2018b; Jackson & Oguro, 2018), defined as "intentional and deliberate pedagogical approaches, activated throughout the study abroad cycle (before, during, and after), that are designed to enhance students' intercultural competence" (Paige & Vande Berg, 2012, pp. 29–30). We would argue that these interventions are equally needed in additional international and transnational higher education contexts. A small number of studies have highlighted the benefits for all students to engage with one another (Jon, 2013; Parsons, 2010). Interventions often include logistical pre-arrival meetings and on-site orientation just after students arrive. It is uncommon for orientations to encompass activities on intercultural communication mixing all students (Wu, Garza, & Guzman, 2015). Rather, if programs include sections on intercultural communication, they tend to be monodirectional: for international students to adapt to the so-called local culture.

A few publications have focused attention on various forms of curriculum interventions. For example, Vande Berg and colleagues (2012) identified seven "defining components" leading to higher intercultural competence. These components primarily revolve around program characteristics, while including individual differences: (1) program length, (2) language competence, (3) use of the language in class, (4) class composition, (5) housing, (6) experiential and cultural learning, and (7) guided reflection. Although some components are not variables that orientation organizers can address or control (e.g., program length and housing), others are addressed by the curriculum, including courses and other components supported by different offices such as student affairs. While language is a common component of intercultural education, its role in fostering intercultural competence has not been widely recognized (Dervin & Liddicoat, 2013). More importantly, language preparations rarely include informal social interactions, even though consideration of multilingual and cultural composition of groups can enhance *languaculture* learning, a term coined by Agar (1994) to remind us that actual language use involves all sorts of cultural knowledge and local information besides just grammar and vocabulary.

A number of interventions have flourished in the form of credit-bearing courses, where students learn about theoretical principles of intercultural communication to support them before, during, or after their intercultural experiences (Jackson, 2017; La Brack, 2016; see also Ene & Cohen, this volume). Successful interventions have included workshops that scaffold explicit intercultural learning, such as using the concept of cultural threads to avoid making essentialist statements (Holliday, 2019); cultural mentoring to help students explore the (host) culture(s) (Paige & Vande Berg, 2012); internationalized first-year writing courses that bring together domestic and international students (Ene & Cohen, this volume); digital storytelling projects (Bush, Allen, Farner, & Pimenova, this volume); and online spaces where students practice intercultural communication skills in intercultural pairings (Rodríguez-Fuentes, Corrales, Paba, & Rosado-Mendinueta, this volume). Additionally, guided critical reflections with regular face-to-face or online feedback (Jackson, 2018a; Passarelli & Kolb, 2012; Savicki & Price, 2019) have become a central component of intercultural growth. Finally, common features of pre-departure or immediate post-arrival activities include meetings with graduates or current international students and lectures on the phases of cross-cultural adaptation that acknowledge that intercultural stays are sometimes challenging.

Nevertheless, efforts to facilitate such learning during the orientation phase—as well as in transnational higher education contexts outside of study abroad programs—have been an overlooked area of investigation. The orientation phase is a particularly salient area of interest because orientations are often viewed as a critical period for setting tone, establishing norms, and beginning relationships that will last for the entirety of students' time at the university (Mullendore & Banahan, 2005; Soria, Lingren Clark, & Coffin Koch, 2013). As a result, DKU has begun thinking critically about how we can use the orientation period to maximize long-term benefits for students' intercultural growth.

DKU Language and Culture Days: An Overview

Informed by a set of best practices, in addition to the default week of orientation, the Language and Culture Days program was added to better prepare students for academic and social environments. In this intervention, we deliberately adopted various practices associated with summer camps to create a short yet memorable and highly interactive experience. Students were grouped into intercultural family groups designed to foster close interactions during learning and exploration. Each day began with a morning rally that included warm-up games and the sharing of photos and videos from the day before. Student Affairs also offered a variety of social activities each night. Key components of Language and Culture Days included:

- Family Groups and Community Exploration
- Story Circles
- Communication between Cultures Workshops
- Reading Strategies and Book Club Sessions
- Community-Based Chinese Language Learning

Family Groups and Community Exploration

Language and Culture Days attempted, over four days of intense social and interactive activities, to address concerns over cultural and linguistic silos on campus by implementing *family groups* for orientation activities. We chose this design to foster sustained intercultural interactions among students and to establish network-like familiarity during orientation. The "family group" label was intended to emphasize commonality and community despite differences. Completing tasks in these groups helped promote mutual understanding and increase students' awareness of culturally diverse approaches to completing academic and non-academic tasks. This experience in turn raised students' awareness of their own unique challenges of adapting to the new internationalized context and positioned students as both experts and learners in terms of their linguistic skills, cultural knowledge, familiarity with academic practices, and knowledge of the local area as they collaborated to complete tasks. We also hoped that this family group approach would help to level perceived power hierarchies and foster more long-term, mutually dependent learning relationships.

In total, we created 22 groups, each comprising 20 students and one faculty or staff mentor, designed to maximize cultural and linguistic diversity. Each group was the core unit for students to complete orientation activities. Recognizing that cultural and linguistic diversity is not exclusively related to nationality, we sought to incorporate the regional diversity of greater China into the groups. For example, family groups were carefully designed to intermix students from various mainland Chinese provinces, Hong Kong, and Taiwan, along with international students from several countries. The rationale behind structuring groups to maximize diversity is supported by research suggesting that intervention is required to develop students' intercultural integration (Davies, 2013) and sociopragmatic competence (Halenko et al., 2019).

Following the LCC's objectives of promoting cultural and language learning, each group was named after an endangered world language, selected by the faculty facilitating orientation. We chose labels from languages around the world, including Quechua (in South America), Mamasani (in Iran), and Maithili (in India/Nepal). This practice provided an interesting theme to explore, raised student awareness of endangered languages, and provided a foundation to promote inclusivity and respect for all cultures in line with the university's core values.

The family group concept served as a thread connecting students and activities throughout the orientation. Each day, during the morning Rise and Shine session, all students would gather collectively, sit with their group, reflect on the previous day's tasks, and learn about upcoming activities. Throughout the day, students would collaborate on academic and language-based tasks, often in family groups, but also at times grouped by linguistic needs. To end each day, groups would reunite to participate in off-campus exploration activities together. They visited a different commercial or cultural site each day and were tasked to complete a video/photographic scavenger hunt together. Scavenger hunt tasks encouraged students to find basic necessities, learn useful terms, identify different restaurants, try local snacks, and create and record a team chant. Upon returning, groups would record new discoveries on a local map and add new words they had learned to a "Words of the World" wall. These activities provided opportunities for students to collaborate outside of traditional academic settings while building familiarity with their new environment. It also gave them a multicultural and multilingual social network from the start of their university studies, even as they went on to develop new friendships after orientation. Several family groups and mentors maintained contact throughout the academic year.

Story Circles

The first activity that new students engaged in during Language and Culture Days was a Story Circle, a research-based methodology designed and piloted by UNESCO to help people in different contexts develop intercultural competence by fostering key skills of "respect, listening, curiosity, self- and other awareness, reflection, sharing, empathy, and relationship building" (Deardorff, 2020, p. 13). This activity capitalizes on the power of storytelling to cultivate three premises: (1) everyone has experiences (stories) to share, (2) everyone can learn from other people, and (3) listening to other people's stories can be transformational (p. 18). Not only can Story Circles have a great impact on learners, they are relatively simple to implement. Story Circles generally operate as follows:

1. Four to six participants sit in a circle.
2. Recommended duration ranges from 75 to 120 minutes.
3. Strict time limits are set for all rounds.
4. Self-introductions: A typical format asks participants to introduce themselves in three words or phrases and explain why those words or phrases are meaningful to them.
5. Storytelling rounds: Participants take turns sharing a story in response to an intercultural prompt (e.g., "What is your earliest memory of difference [when you first learned or realized that you were different from someone else]?"

Deardorff, 2020, p. 35), while others listen for understanding without interrupting the storyteller.

6. Flashbacks: After each storytelling round, everyone listens without interruption as each listener shares something they found memorable about each story, ensuring that all stories receive flashbacks.

7. Reflection: Reflection questions ask participants to discuss common themes they noticed in the stories, things that surprised or challenged them, what they learned about themselves by taking part in the activity, or how the experience may affect their future actions.

In DKU's Language and Culture Days, Story Circles were employed on the first day, immediately following icebreakers within family groups. The LCC director introduced the activity, emphasizing the importance of practicing non-judgmental listening (i.e., listening for understanding, Deardorff, 2020) and maintaining confidentiality through the following guidelines:

- ○ Really listen to everyone else.
- ○ Don't interrupt others.
- ○ Make sure everyone gets to speak.
- ○ Don't talk too long. Keep it simple, clear, and focused.
- ○ Listen and speak respectfully.
- ○ Be positive and constructive.
- ○ Be yourself—speak just from your own experience.
- ○ Maintain confidentiality—don't talk outside the group about what people inside your group said.

The family group mentors then divided their families into smaller groups of approximately five students each. After confirming that students understood how to proceed, the facilitators left the room. This allowed the students to feel comfortable sharing their stories with one another and made it possible for intercultural learning to take place without interference from mentors (Borghetti & Beaven, 2018). During this activity, students practiced applying the non-judgmental listening skills introduced at the start of the session, which facilitators reminded students to practice throughout the remainder of Language and Culture Days activities.

Communicating between Cultures Workshops

During the remaining three days of Language and Culture Days, LCC faculty teams facilitated a series of 90-minute workshops called "Communicating between Cultures" (CBC). These workshops were intended to raise awareness of factors that can influence intercultural interactions and teach strategies that students could use to mitigate negative experiences. Facilitators worked together from a shared set of goals to develop lesson plans for the three workshops. A thematic concept that structured these workshops was the "birds of a feather" phenomenon—the tendency for people in diverse cultural environments to gravitate toward similar individuals. The intention was not to discourage this form of self-sorting but to make students aware of the phenomenon. The workshops also encouraged students to seek out diversity and attempted to equip them with concepts and strategies that could facilitate their engagement in DKU's intercultural environment.

CBC workshops were held in four large groups of 80–85 students each and typically began by dividing students into smaller groups for discussions of a critical (intercultural) incident, a realistic scenario that includes an example of intercultural miscommunication (Pederson, 1995; Wight, 1995). The incident discussed during the first workshop was "Left out of the Conversation," in which a Chinese student from a Chinese university struggles to feel included by his international classmates in the casual environment of a bar (Snow, 2014). Small groups of students brainstormed possible explanations for why this feeling of exclusion occurred, attempting to consider more and less charitable explanations for the behaviors and motivations of the Chinese student and his classmates. Representatives from each group reported their ideas before a whole-group debriefing session. Students then evaluated the likelihood of these explanations and discussed strategies for over-coming the issues. From these practical discussions, facilitators could then generalize to a series of phenomena in intercultural interactions and offer their own experience in confronting similar situations.

Reading Strategies and Book Club Sessions

Chinese students from the 2018–2019 academic year expressed anxiety over their ability to satisfy course reading requirements (approximately 40–50 pages of reading a week per course) and, subsequently, related course assignments. Furthermore, while Chinese students admitted to DKU have the English language abilities required for academic study, many have never had to carry an English language reading load consistent with the expectations of academic study at the university, raising concerns about their abilities to comprehend and engage with readings to succeed in course requirements and assessments across the university. These concerns led to the incorporation of a daily intervention, including 75-minute sessions fostering active reading strategies for all EAP-track students. These sessions were followed by daily 60-minute book club meetings with family group members and mentors to share culturally diverse perspectives on the readings and foster good discussion habits.

The sessions taught students useful metacognitive and cognitive reading strategies by reading selected chapters from Malcolm Gladwell's (2008) *Outliers: The Story of Success* in a limited time frame. This popular non-fiction text was chosen for its accessibility, readability, and thought-provoking content. The general purpose of these sessions was to model getting the essence of a reading assignment during the semester, with four instructional goals:

1. Teach one practical reading strategy daily, including pre-reading strategies before reading an entire text, to initiate students into the habit of applying reading strategies.
2. Demonstrate how reading texts word-by-word is an ineffective reading method.

3. Model time management for academic reading.
4. Provide a challenging but positive experience reading an authentic English language text.

The 75-minute sessions were divided into three parts and began with a whole-group introduction to the reading strategy for 5–10 minutes. Next was independent reading time for students to apply the reading strategy to the assigned chapter for one hour. During reading time, faculty circulated to provide support and clarification. Sessions ended with a whole-group debrief of five minutes to review conversation strategies.

The framework for the active reading strategies sessions was introduced to the students as a series of practical solutions to realistic challenges. These solutions include strategies for purposefully reading lengthy English language texts with unfamiliar vocabulary items for multiple courses; overcoming feelings of discouragement during reading; and resisting the use of translation applications (e.g., Baidu Translate) for reading texts, and instead using co-text, context, and interactional strategies to decipher meaning (Nuttall, 2005, p. 17). Students were encouraged to remember that reading comprehension and vocabulary acquisition are skills that develop over time with consistent attention and practice. For each reading strategy taught, students were tasked with applying it to an assigned chapter that had corresponding discussion questions that would be used later each day in the Book Club sessions. This motivated students to engage with the daily reading strategies so that they could actively participate in Book Club discussions. These reading strategies were practiced with *Outliers:*

1. *Skimming:* Students began to develop efficiency-maximizing strategies to enable a large task to become manageable. With a reading load of approximately 30–50 pages per hour, this strategy helped prepare students for realistic university reading loads.

2. *Skimming and question-forming:* Students engaged in critical thinking, predicting, and further activating schemata to

enhance effective comprehension in preparedness for critical discussion during Book Club sessions.

3. *Note-taking:* Students practiced engaging critically with the text, identifying, summarizing, and responding to key ideas in preparation for discussions.

4. *Showing what you know:* Students worked collaboratively to discuss and exemplify effective comprehension, further building confidence for participation and engagement in Book Club discussions.

International students completed readings independently, and in the afternoon, family groups reconvened with their mentors to establish a regular, comfortable space around campus to hold Book Club sessions. Led by mentors using a pre-designed template of open questions, Book Club sessions facilitated an exchange of culturally diverse ideas and perspectives on the chapters. Furthermore, they provided a useful opportunity for students to practice discussion skills, introduced through gambits during the reading strategies sessions and supplemented by good discussion guidelines. Student engagement and participation were partially managed and input was elicited if required, but discussion often became student-initiated and led to critical thinking and presentation of conflicting perspectives.

Research has explored the link between reading narrative fiction and developing empathy (McCreary & Marchant, 2017; Oatley, 2016; Yates, 2020). Although *Outliers* is non-fiction, it still required students to understand the emotions of the chapters' various protagonists through perspective-taking. Perhaps more importantly, as Book Club discussions took place within the multicultural family groups, students had opportunities to hear perspectives and experiences both different from and similar to their own. This sharing allowed for greater intercultural understanding and empathy than could have been gained from reading the text independently. For example, while discussing Gladwell's claims about factors leading to success and drawing connections to the popular notion of "grit," students in some family groups shared and compared their high school experiences. Some students expressed surprise at differences in the length of a school day or the number and kinds of classes taken, while others commented on similarities with peers from other countries.

In terms of developing students' L2 reading skills, optimal, systematic, and deliberate practice has been shown to facilitate L2 skill acquisition (Suzuki, Nakata, & Dekeyser, 2019), with Grabe (2016) reporting that increased practice can promote L1 and L2 reading fluency. Recognizing that the reading load for DKU courses would be greater than most incoming students were used to, we therefore aimed to engage students in deliberate reading practice with meaningful intercultural follow-up discussion from the very start of their undergraduate program. These sessions provided a foundation for continued work in reading and discussion strategies in the first-year EAP courses.

Community-Based Chinese Language Learning

As a counterpart to the Active Reading Strategies sessions designed for EAP-track students, Chinese language sessions were built into the program for CSL-track students. Sixty percent of the incoming international students had no prior Chinese learning experience and were assigned to the Daily Life Chinese group. The remaining 40 percent, who came with varying levels of Chinese language proficiency and cultural understanding, were assigned to the RealLife Practice group. These sessions were grounded in the performed culture approach (PCA) proposed by Walker (2000) for foreign language teaching, which treats language and culture as an inseparable unit inside and outside classroom settings. The Chinese language sessions aimed to optimize the learning opportunities offered by real-life encounters in the local context for international first-year students. These sessions had four primary goals:

1. Motivate students to think of Chinese learning as practice to gain skills to enrich their multicultural experience in China.
2. Help students build knowledge and connections on and off campus in the local community by using Chinese to navigate social scenarios central to their college lives.

3. Cultivate a communal culture of language learning among students of different linguistic and cultural backgrounds.

4. Respond to individual learning needs of CSL learners at different levels, especially for the Real Life Practice group.

To achieve these goals, this intervention was informed by Kolb's (1984) experiential learning cycle. A full instructional cycle for the Chinese language sessions included these steps:

1. During the morning session, students learned and practiced target linguistic performances in authentic scenarios appropriate to their language proficiency levels.

2. During the afternoon of the same day, international students collaborated with Chinese peers to practice the target language in authentic contexts with Chinese speakers on and off campus.

3. Students used a task sheet to record their actual performance and information or linguistic items collected and wrote a short reflection on their efforts.

4. Students reported in class the next day to receive feedback.

In designing the language tasks, we prioritized contexts that are most relevant to DKU students' daily encounters, such as ordering food at the Chinese cafeteria, using local transportation to go to the mall, and conducting small talk with a taxi driver. Combining these language tasks with the scavenger hunt activities, students were able to complete their language tasks with Chinese students from their family group on the same explorative trip. To foster peer learning and general communication across cultural groups, we intentionally designed tasks that require engagement in Chinese with Chinese students, such as introducing oneself to a Chinese student in the same family group and getting to know them better, or inviting a Chinese student to observe one's conversation with local people and give feedback for improvement. Supported by one or two designated faculty mentors in each subgroup, students in the Real Life group built their own script and were given the flexibility to pick from a few well-defined language tasks that best fit their individual interests and skill levels. Compared with the true beginner Daily Life group, planning for the Real Life group faced the additional challenge of accommodating and engaging Chinese learners ranging from low-intermediate to advanced levels who had diverse Chinese learning interests and backgrounds. The availability of a range of tasks that required varied levels of linguistic skills and cultural capacities kept the whole Real Life group engaged by challenging the students at different levels to individually stretch their Chinese skills as needed.

From a holistic perspective, the Chinese language sessions were designed to bridge students' Chinese language learning journey in the next four years at DKU. Through intercultural peer-learning, active participation in the local community from day 1, and individualized learning experiences that foster a vision of themselves as Chinese language users, we promoted a specific orientation toward Chinese language learning at DKU: Learning Chinese means more than getting good grades in required CSL courses. Instead, it means becoming better at accomplishing communicative tasks in the community and connecting with people toward shared goals.

Student Feedback/Evaluation

How did we determine the effectiveness of the program? We have two sources of student feedback. The first is an online student evaluation of the 2019 DKU undergraduate orientation co-administered by the Office of Student Affairs and the Assessment Office via Qualtrics. We used the portion of the survey related to the Language and Culture Days, which solicited students' comments on the helpfulness of the program, what worked well and what should be improved, and further suggestions they might have. A total of 184 students responded to the survey. The second source is a paper-based exit survey administered at the last Chinese Real Life Practice session. This survey, completed by 24 students, asked participants to list the most memorable tasks conducted during the Chinese language session and outside the classroom and what they gained from participating in the tasks.

The student feedback suggests effectiveness of the design of the Language and Culture Days in three areas. First, in terms of community-building and cross-cultural integration, out of the 184 students who participated in the undergraduate orientation survey, the vast majority believed that the Language and Culture Days helped them "gain a better understanding of communication between cultures" (95.6 percent) and "establish friendship with students from a variety of backgrounds" (94 percent). Second, in terms of promoting students' academic and second language development, the vast majority of student respondents reported that the orientation programs helped them "feel comfortable with group discussion" (97 percent) and that they were "better prepared for language learning at DKU" (95.7 percent). Third, students also recognized that the Language and Culture Days programming highlighted the integration of both intercultural and academic/second language development. The top three gains reported by students who participated in the Chinese Real Life Practice session were that they "learned new linguistic items or authentic expressions" (91 percent), "started to build social relationships with Chinese students on campus" (87 percent), and "practiced doing things in Chinese in community of Kunshan" (78 percent).

Implications for Internationalization in Higher Education

The dramatic growth of internationalization in higher education has led to the need for innovative intercultural programs such as Language and Culture Days. As this is a new and developing program, we only have limited data such as student evaluations and observations to evaluate the full benefits, but we have learned much from developing and implementing it. For example, because orientations provide an ideal opportunity to engage students from the very start of their undergraduate degree program, we firmly believe they are a viable intervention to overcome the immersion myth and the associated challenges of developing students' intercultural competence and on-campus cross-cultural integration. We have evaluated the strengths and limitations of the

Language and Culture Days program and reflected on our experiences based on observation and student evaluation; we offer a few insights that may inspire others looking to develop similar intercultural orientation programs.

○ One of the primary goals of the interventionist design was fostering community-building and integration across the student body. The orientation activities maximized student collaboration with peers of different cultural backgrounds via local exploration, community- and strategy-based language tasks and practices, and intercultural awareness education. The implementation of family groups as units of operation throughout the orientation encouraged first-year students to quickly establish relationships rooted in a variety of shared experiences and achievement of common goals. As indicated in the student evaluations of the orientation activities, these relationships extended across commonly perceived cultural boundaries.

○ Another strength of the program was that faculty and staff of DKU representing diverse intercultural expertise and backgrounds modeled the types and depth of interactions and collaboration in a multilingual and multicultural context. For instance, EAP faculty members who are proficient speakers and experienced learners of Mandarin were the ones to lead Daily Life and Real Life Chinese sessions with CSL faculty. Such collaborative efforts are also evident in the way different orientation activities were designed to build on one another in fostering transferable skills, such as the reading strategies sessions and Book Club, as well as the Chinese language sessions and the daily local excursions. In response to incoming students' lack of readiness for the new transnational academic context, the orientation activities included learning and motivational strategies that support the EAP and CSL curricula during the academic year. These included reading and discussion strategies for EAP-track students and contextualized performance-oriented language learning for

CSL-track students, which were evaluated positively by the students.

○ One note of reflection for future programming is that, although language sessions were designed to be reinforced and expanded on in the regular semester, we were limited by the short timeframe of the four-day orientation. We remain concerned whether the foundational effects of the orientation will endure if they are not supported by institutional reinforcements throughout the year—a concern that has only deepened as a result of the COVID-19 pandemic, which has scattered the student body around the world. As Jackson (2018a) warns, orientations by themselves provide insufficient support. A successful internationalized education requires continued efforts in providing well-designed and complementary interventions. A longitudinal assessment of students' intercultural competence and performance beyond this initial intervention would provide a full picture of students' experiences and needs in the context of joint-venture universities in China and better inform future pedagogical practices.

○ Overall, the orientation program provided students with a positive, authentic platform to develop their intercultural, language, and academic skills, as well as the means to network and familiarize themselves with a diverse group of peers in a camp-like atmosphere. By forging bonds through regular collaboration to complete tasks in family groups both on and off campus, students were able to enter their undergraduate programs with an intercultural peer support network. While we do not yet know the long-term sustainable effects on students' intercultural development, based on our post-orientation observations and student feedback, the orientation program was a success.

Although the program presented in this chapter was designed with DKU in mind, the goals, key concepts, and general format should be easily adaptable to other higher education contexts. Finally, while we are aware there is no one solution for all situations, we would argue that incorporating research-based best practices into orientation programs provides students with increased chances for long-term success.

Acknowledgment of Contribution

All co-authors contributed equally to this chapter. Author names are listed in alphabetical order.

References

Agar, M. (1994). Language shock: Understanding the culture of conversation. New York: William Morrow.

Block, D. (2007). Second language identities. London: Continuum.

Borghetti, C., & Beaven, A. (2018). Monitoring class interaction to maximize intercultural learning in mobility contexts. In J. Jackson & S. Oguro (Eds.), Intercultural interventions in study abroad (pp. 37–54). New York: Routledge.

Brewer, E., & Moore, J. (2015). Where and how do students learn abroad? In V. Savicki & E. Brewer (Eds.), Assessing study abroad: Theory, tools, and practice (pp. 145–161). Sterling, VA: Stylus.

Caruana, V., & Montgomery, C. (2015). Understanding the transnational higher education landscape: Shifting positionality and the complexities of partnership. Learning and Teaching, 8(1), 5–29. http://dx.doi.org/10.3167/latiss.2015.080102

Davies, J. A. (2013). A preliminary investigation into the major concerns of Chinese students preparing to study abroad: A practical approach to facilitating student transition. English Teaching in China, 2, 6–12. http://etic.xjtlu.edu.cn/PDF/issue_02/davies_2013.pdf

Deardorff, D. K. (2006). Identification and assessment of intercultural competence as a student outcome of internationalization. Journal of Studies in International Education, 10, 241–266.

Deardorff, D. K. (2020). Manual for developing intercultural competencies: Story circles. New York: Routledge.

Dervin, F., & Liddicoat, A. J. (2013). Introduction: Linguistics for intercultural education. In F. Dervin & A. J. Liddicoat (Eds.), Language Learning & Language Teaching (pp. 1–25). Amsterdam: John Benjamins Publishing Company. https://doi.org/10.1075/lllt.33.01der

Gladwell, M. (2008) *Outliers: The story of success.* New York: Little, Brown and Company.

Grabe, W. (2016). Fluency in reading: Thirty-five years later. *Reading in a Foreign Language, 22*(1), 77–83.

Gurin, P., Day, E. L., Hurtado, S., & Gurin, G. (2002). Diversity and higher education: Theory and impact on educational outcomes. *Harvard Educational Review, 72*(3), 330–366.

Halenko, N., Jones, C., Davies, L., & Davies, J. (2019). Surveying pragmatic performance during a study abroad stay: A cross-sectional look at the language of spoken requests. *Intercultural Communication Education, 2*(2), 71–87. https://doi.org/10.29140/ice.v2n2.162

Holliday, A. (2019). *Understanding intercultural communication: Negotiating a grammar of culture* (2nd ed.). London: Routledge.

Institute of International Education. (2019). *U.S. study abroad.* Retrieved from https://www.iie.org/en/Research-and-Insights/Open-Doors/Data/US-Study-Abroad

Jackson, J. (2015). Becoming interculturally competent: Theory to practice in international education. *International Journal of Intercultural Relations, 48,* 91–107. https://doi.org/10.1016/j.ijintrel.2015.03.012

Jackson, J. (2017). Intervening in the intercultural learning of L2 study abroad students: From research to practice. *Language Teaching, 51*(3), 365–382. https://doi.org/10.1017/S0261444816000392

Jackson, J. (2018a). Optimizing intercultural learning and engagement abroad through online mentoring. In J. Jackson & S. Oguro (Eds.), *Intercultural interventions in study abroad* (pp. 119–136). London: Routledge.

Jackson, J. (2018b). *Interculturality in international education.* New York: Routledge.

Jackson, J., & Oguro, S. (2018). Introduction: Enhancing and extending study abroad learning through intercultural interventions. In J. Jackson & S. Oguro (Eds.), *Intercultural interventions in study abroad* (pp. 1–17). London: Routledge.

Jon, J.-E. (2013). Realizing internationalization at home in Korean higher education: Promoting domestic students' interaction with international students and intercultural competence. *Journal of Studies in International Education, 17*(4), 455–470. https://doi.org/10.1177/1028315312468329

Kinginger, C. (2009). *Language learning and study abroad: A critical reading of research.* Basingstoke, England: Palgrave Macmillan.

Knight, J. (2015). International universities: Misunderstandings and emerging models? *Journal of Studies in International Education, 19*(2), 107–121. https://doi.org/10.1177/1028315315572899

Kolb, D. A. (1984). *Experiential learning: Experience as the source of learning and development* (Vol. 1). Englewood Cliffs, NJ: Prentice-Hall.

La Brack, B. (2016). The interplay and co-evolution of theory and practice in preparing students for international education experiences: A retrospective analysis. In B. Streitweiser & A. C. Ogden (Eds.), *International higher education's scholar-practitioners: Bridging research and practice* (pp. 169–182). Oxford, England: Symposium Books.

McCreary, J. J., Marchant, G. J. (2017). Reading and Empathy. *Reading Psychology, 38(2),* 182–202. https://doi.org/10.1080/02702711.2016.1245690

Mullendore, R. H., & Banahan, L. A. (2005). Designing orientation programs. In M. Lee Upcraft, J. N. Gardner, & B. O. Barefoot, & Associates (Eds.), *Challenging and supporting the first-year student: A handbook for improving the first year of college* (pp. 391–409). San Francisco: Jossey-Bass.

Nuttall, C. (2005) *Teaching reading skills in a foreign language.* Oxford, England: Macmillan.

Oatley, K. (2016). Fiction: Simulation of social worlds. *Trends in Cognitive Sciences, 20*(8), 618–628. https://doi.org/10.1016/j.tics.2016.06.002

Ogden, A. C., & Brewer, E. (2019). U.S. education abroad: Historical perspectives, emerging trends, and changing narratives. In E. Brewer & A. C. Ogden (Eds.), *Education abroad and the undergraduate experience: Critical perspectives and approaches to integration with student learning and development* (pp. 15–40). Sterling, VA: Stylus.

Otten, M. (2003). Intercultural learning and diversity in higher education. *Journal of Studies in International Education, 7*(1), 12–26. https://doi.org/10.1177/1028315302250177

Paige, R. M., & Vande Berg, M. (2012). Why students are not learning abroad. In M. Vande Berg, M. Paige, & K. H. Lou (Eds.), *Students learning abroad: What our students are learning, what they're not, and what we can do about it* (pp. 29–58). Sterling, VA: Stylus.

Parsons, R. L. (2010). The effects of an internationalized university experience on domestic students in the United States and Australia. *Journal of Studies in International Education, 14,* 313–334. https://doi.org/10.1177/1028315309331390

Passarelli, A., & Kolb, D. A. (2012). Using experiential learning theory to promote student learning and development in programs of education abroad. In M. Vande Berg, R. M. Paige, & K. H. Lou (Eds.), *Students learning abroad: What our students are learning, what they're not, and what we can do about it* (pp. 137–161). Sterling, VA: Stylus.

Pederson, P. (1995). *The five stages of culture shock: Critical incidents around the world.* Westport, CT: Greenwood Press.

Savicki, V., & Price, M. V. (2019). Reflection as a tool in the educational continuum. In E. Brewer & A. C. Ogden (Eds.), *Education abroad and the undergraduate experience: Critical perspectives and approaches to integration with student learning and development* (pp. 165–180). Sterling, VA: Stylus.

Snow, D. (2014). *Encounters with Westerners: Improving skills in English and intercultural communication* (Rev. ed.). Shanghai, PRC: Shanghai Foreign Language Education Press.

Soria, K., Lingren Clark, B., & Coffin Koch, L. (2013). Investigating the academic and social benefits of extended new student orientations for first-year students. *Journal of College Orientation and Transition, 20*(2), 33–45.

Suzuki, Y., Nakata, T., & Dekeyser, R. (2019). The desirable difficulty framework as a theoretical foundation for optimizing and researching second language practice. *The Modern Language Journal, 103*(3), 713–720.

Terzuolo, E. R. (2018). Intercultural development in study abroad: Influence of student and program characteristics. *International Journal of Intercultural Relations, 65,* 86–95. https://doi.org/10.1016/j.ijintrel.2018.05.001

Vande Berg, M., Paige, R. M., & Lou, K. (Eds.). (2012). *Student learning abroad: What our students are learning, what they're not, and what we can do about it.* Sterling, VA: Stylus.

Walker, G. (2000). Performed culture: Learning to participate in another culture. In R. D. Lambert & E. Shohamy (Eds.), *Language policy and pedagogy* (p. 221). Philadelphia: John Benjamins. https://doi.org/10.1075/z.96.14wal

Wight, A. R. (1995). The critical incident as a training tool. In S. M. Fowler (Ed.), *Intercultural sourcebook: Cross-cultural training methods* (Vol. 1, pp. 127–140). Yarmouth, ME: Intercultural Press.

Wu, H.-P., Garza, E., & Guzman, N. (2015). International student's challenge and adjustment to college. *Education Research International,* Article ID 202753, 9 pages, https://doi.org/10.1155/2015/202753

Yates, J. N. (2020). Literature and racial social sensitivity at a rural two-year community college. (Publication No. 8626). Unpublished doctoral diss., University of Oklahoma, Norman. https://hdl.handle.net/11244/324310

2

Developing a Language Center for International Students: Benefits, Strategies, and Challenges

Cristine McMartin-Miller

International students are a key part of internationalization efforts at many colleges and universities in the United States, and the value and benefits that they bring to these institutions of higher education and their communities are well documented. In a study of faculty perceptions of international students, Jin and Schneider (2019) found that faculty believed that international students perform better academically than domestic students, bring diverse and different views to class, and contribute to campus multilingualism. In a survey of alumni, Luo and Jamieson-Drake (2013) found that domestic students who interacted extensively with international students had higher levels of engagement in college activities than peers who had had less interaction. Trice (2003) reported that faculty believed international graduate students enhanced domestic students' learning experience by providing a more global perspective. Participants in Trice's study also noted international graduate students' high academic quality, leading them to fill many research assistantships. According to one faculty member, "They [international graduate students] keep our program going. You've got to have graduate students to have research" (Trice, 2003, p. 393). Similarly, Hegarty (2014) described how doctoral programs have grown in response to demand from international students, and, at the institutional level, international students are actively recruited because most pay full tuition (Qureshi & Khawaja, 2021). The economic impact of international students in the United States is, in fact, enormous. According to a National Association for Foreign Student Affairs (NAFSA) analysis of the 2019–2020 academic year, international students contributed $38.7 billion and 415,996 jobs to the U.S. economy (NAFSA, 2020). In Massachusetts, the context of this chapter, the same report estimated that international students had contributed $3.2 billion and 36,076 jobs (NAFSA, 2020).

With these positive contributions come challenges for this large and diverse population, including English language proficiency, academic acculturation, culture shock, financial concerns, social isolation, and homesickness (Andrade et al., 2014; Billedo et al., 2020; Gautam et al., 2016; Kuo, 2011). Jones and Young (2020) found that, during their college years, international students are less likely than their domestic peers to thrive in such areas as engaged learning, positive perspective, and social connectedness. For their part, faculty are often aware of such issues but feel unsure or conflicted about how to deal with them in their teaching (Jin & Schneider, 2019). Unfortunately, this research is not necessarily being used by faculty and administrators to drive practice (Özturgut and Murphy, 2009). As Knight (2011) argued, "[a] longstanding myth is that more foreign students on campus will produce more internationalized culture and curriculum" (p. 15). In other words, institutions of higher learning must take intentional actions to ensure that international students are adequately positioned for success.

How, then, can universities and colleges best support international students? Options include not only academic courses but also what Leask (2015) calls the *informal curriculum,* which she defines as "various support services and additional activities and options organized by the university that are not assessed and don't form a part of the formal curriculum" (p. 8). In this chapter, I describe the development of one such space: the International Tutoring Center (ITC) at Northeastern University. I first address the need to distinguish the ITC from other campus services, such as the Writing Center, and then provide an overview of the ITC and the strategies that have contributed to its success—including offering tutorials across a range of skills and multiple modalities, employing a staff of highly trained tutors, promoting the ITC, and strategic partnerships with other university offices—as well as challenges that have arisen. Ultimately, the purpose of this chapter is to demonstrate that the ITC and other centers that exclusively serve international students are uniquely positioned to meet international students' holistic needs and that, by contributing to international students' success, the university benefits as a whole.

The International Tutoring Center

Northeastern University's location in the heart of Boston makes it an appealing destination for international students. Larger cities are generally more attractive to international students (Qureshi & Khawaja, 2021), and famously walkable Boston offers easy access to many historical, cultural, and sporting attractions. Its reputation as a hub of higher education is also known throughout the world: with 44 colleges and universities in the metropolitan area, Boston is sometimes called "America's College Town."

Among these institutions, Northeastern University is distinguished by its sizable international student population. In 2020, the Institute of International Education identified the Boston campus as hosting the second highest number of international students among all colleges and universities in the United States. With 11,700 international students from 140 countries, international students account for approximately one-third of the student body at Northeastern (Northeastern University, 2020b).

At Northeastern University, much of the support—formal and informal—for international students is offered through NU Global, a unit within the College of Professional Studies. NU Global houses robust undergraduate and graduate pathway programs and Global Student Success (GSS). According to its website, "GSS is dedicated to helping international students and non-native English speakers, as well as scholars, faculty, and staff at Northeastern, through a variety of services and resources" (Northeastern University, 2020a). In this way, the voluntary programs of GSS align with *Northeastern 2025*, the university's academic plan. In it, students are promised the opportunity to participate in "just-for-you learning" designed to support independent learning goals (Northeastern University, 2016). This plan also reiterates the benefits of a diverse student population, stating, "Learning networks of diverse ideas, experiences, and perspectives—activated by inclusiveness—strengthen professional, intellectual, and cultural agility. They transform globalization from a challenge to an opportunity" (Northeastern University, 2016). Within GSS, this specifically includes: language and culture workshops; reading workshops; a listening and speaking course; training for faculty and staff; and the focus of this chapter, the ITC.

Open to all Northeastern international students—as well as international faculty and staff—the ITC provides free, comprehensive English language instruction from professional tutors. It has proved to be a popular co-curricular space among Northeastern's international students, but it took years of intentional, collaborative action to achieve this.

When the ITC was founded in 2009, it was originally conceived as a writing center for international students and staffed primarily with tutors with backgrounds in first language composition. In 2012, NU Global administrators decided that the ITC would expand its scope to offer tutorials in language skills beyond writing. This expansion was motivated by a desire to meet administrators' perceived student needs (no formal needs assessment was conducted) and to further distinguish the ITC from the university writing center.

Currently, the ITC offers ten tutorial types. These include: conversation, pronunciation, reading, presentation skills, TOEFL® preparation, and career preparation tutorials; writing tutorials are divided into sub-skills, including planning, organization, grammar, and citations. Of these, conversation is the most popular, followed by career preparation and grammar. In the spring of 2021, for example, appointments for these skill areas accounted for 50, 15, and 15 percent of all appointments, respectively.

In addition to addressing an array of skills, the ITC offers four formats: face-to-face one-on-one tutorials; online one-on-one tutorials; and face-to-face group tutorials; and online group tutorials. Online tutorials were introduced in part to allow students at Northeastern's satellite campuses—there are now eight across the United States, Canada, and England—to use the ITC. Group tutorials, in which one tutor meets with up to four students, were introduced to encourage students who were hesitant to visit the ITC independently to go with a friend or to accommodate students who wanted to work on group projects. Group tutorials also allow more students' access to tutorials. Students can make up to two 50-minute appointments of any type per week at the ITC, but as the popularity of the ITC has grown, appointments can be difficult to get.

In another attempt to increase access, we have experimented with additional locations. The original ITC is located in the basement of the Boston main campus library. In the fall of 2014, a satellite center at the smaller downtown Boston campus was established. A third branch of the ITC at Northeastern's Seattle campus opened in the fall of 2015. Both satellite locations, however, have since been closed (the latter due to administrative restructuring and the former due to its lower utilization rate).

Another element that has changed over the years is oversight of the ITC. While there was initially faculty supervision of the tutors, an academic advisor had assumed this role when I joined NU Global in 2012. He reported to the assistant director of GSS, who in turn, reported to the director. Hired as faculty, I first provided informal guidance to the ITC to address the recently added skills by assisting in the hiring of additional tutors with expertise in these areas and offering workshops to train current tutors. In 2013, I was formally assigned the role of program coordinator of the ITC and, with a course release equaling 1/16 of my workload, assumed oversight of the pedagogical aspects of the center. This included the continued recruitment and training of ITC tutors, as well as working with GSS to develop ITC policies. I also inherited many administrative tasks, such as creating the schedule each semester and onboarding new tutors.

In 2016, a new director of GSS was hired, and she soon led several initiatives to improve the ITC. To make the physical space more modern and comfortable for clients and staff, the new director began a beautification effort, including the removal of bulky computer stations and adding vertical dividers designed to decrease noise. Both served to address a common complaint among ITC tutors: that the space was too noisy and cramped. The new director also put a focus on publicity and outreach to increase awareness of the ITC across campus. These efforts have included: introducing the ITC at student orientations, staffing informational displays about ITC services at the Student Center, distributing physical and digital flyers, adding content about ITC services to university announcements, updating the website, and creating a stronger social media presence. Meanwhile, I wrote a curriculum for class visits and an overview of ITC services for all NU Global syllabi. This variety of promotional efforts seemed to be effective. Internal surveys of ITC awareness among NU Global faculty and staff indicated that participants are not only familiar with the service but also regularly recommend it to their students.

The new director also successfully lobbied for the creation of the first full-time ITC position, and in 2018, an English Language Specialist (ELS) was hired. The responsibilities of the ELS include not only tutoring but also overseeing daily operations of the center, planning and implementing workshops, promoting GSS services, developing partnerships with other offices that support international students, and serving as a liaison between the tutors and GSS. Because evening and weekend appointments are popular among students but difficult to staff, the ELS works an off-set schedule of 10 am to 6 pm Tuesday through Saturday. This position made it possible for the ITC to address the most frequent student complaint about the ITC—that there are no available appointment slots. Although students can sign up for appointments two weeks in advance, slots fill up quickly. With the arrival of the ELS, ITS is able to open four hours of "same-day" tutorials each morning.

These changes in GSS staffing decreased and eventually eliminated the administrative duties I had been fulfilling as program coordinator of the ITC. Since then, and with an increase in course release, I am now able to focus more on tutor training and ITC research, some of which I detail in a later section.

As a result of these very collaborative efforts to expand the ITC, usage exploded. In the fall of 2012, there were approximately 200 appointments. In contrast, in the spring of 2020, there were 2,008 appointments, an incredible increase of 1,004 percent. According to data collected through the web-based scheduling system WCONLINE during that time, graduate students comprised the vast majority (82 percent) of ITC users, most of whom were students in the College of Engineering (31 percent) or the College of Professional Studies (27 percent). The most commonly spoken first or native language among ITC users was Mandarin Chinese (65 percent). Internal research has revealed additional information about users. For example, an analysis of visitation found that Pathways students (i.e., those conditionally admitted to the university pending completion of English language courses) who visited the ITC had higher grade point averages (3.52/4.00) than those who had not (3.36/4.00).

Why are students visiting? Additional internal research suggests that students visit the ITC for more than just language skills. For instance, a survey of tutors indicated that they believed many students visit the ITC because they are lonely. Interviews of students in another internal study also found that students are attracted to the welcoming environment. Said one participant, "I remember a specific time when I entered the center, and the tutors inside, they know me and greeted to me. That made me feel so happy and satisfied. Kind of a little bit proud of myself." Indeed, the ITC enjoys a positive reputation among its users. According to 257 anonymous satisfaction surveys completed in the spring of 2021, 95 percent of respondents said they "strongly agreed" and 5 percent said they "agreed" that they would recommend the ITC. That 55 percent of visitors made three or more appointments during that time frame—some "super users" made around 100 appointments per year—also indicates that international students value the ITC.

Elements of a Successful Language Center

The primary reason for the ITC's success is, of course, its tutors. These professional tutors further serve to differentiate the ITC from the university writing center, where peer/student tutors are employed. To work at the ITC, the minimum qualifications include a bachelor's degree or higher in a relevant field (e.g., TESOL or linguistics) and at least two years teaching or tutoring international students at the post-secondary level. In reality, the tutors have always exceeded these qualifications. For instance, all but one of the current 12 tutors have a master's degree or higher.

Another factor that has contributed to center success is sustained tutor training. One of the first major projects I led as coordinator was the creation of a tutor handbook formalizing ITC policies and procedures. I relied on a model generously provided by the Northeastern Writing Center, as well as literature in second language studies and ESL tutoring guidebooks (e.g., Bruce & Rafoth, 2009; Babcock & Thonus, 2018), to incorporate suggested practices for tutorials, such as that tutors are advised to prioritize global concerns and provide students with self-editing strategies rather than proofread. To sustain continuity of practice, the tutor handbook is regularly revised and was reviewed by our human resources department and university counsel; tutors must attest that they are familiar with its content annually. We also require new tutors to observe two tutorials as part of their onboarding process. All of these actions help us ensure that students can expect to encounter a consistent, high level of service every time they visit the ITC.

Although tutor training was initially focused on orienting new tutors, time is dedicated at each monthly staff meeting for professional development. We also hold bi-annual ITC retreats, three-hour events that always incorporate an element of training. Topics for this training are based on tutor requests or reflect emerging needs. Recent topics include updated APA guidelines and best practices for conducting online tutorials.

Tutor training is also informed by internal research of the ITC. For instance, when an internal survey found that students may avoid tutorials because they are embarrassed about their English or shy, I introduced training about reducing anxiety during tutorials. Suggested strategies for addressing this issue included providing easily comprehensible input, increasing "wait time" after questions, negotiating with students how feedback will be delivered, discussing tutors' own language learning challenges, and emphasizing that the ITC is a safe environment.

Formal evaluation of tutors further ensures that best practices are being implemented. These annual evaluations draw from a variety of sources, including a tutor self-assessment, student satisfaction surveys, participation in staff meetings, and peer observations. GSS staff and I create a report for each tutor, and the ELS and I meet with them individually to collect feedback from them, as well. Through this comprehensive process, we are able to acknowledge tutors' performance, identify areas in need of improvement, and refine the operations of the ITC as a whole.

Increasingly, tutor training has focused less on language and more on how the ITC can holistically support international students at Northeastern. Tutors generally have a pulse on current issues of concern to international students, and many develop very close relationships with students. During tutorials, students sometimes disclose personal issues, such as depression or sexual harassment, which tutors are not qualified to address. A recent retreat therefore featured a presentation by an ITC tutor on mental health challenges specific to international students. So that tutors can refer students to the appropriate resource, we have also begun inviting representatives from various campus entities to provide overviews of their services. This has included presentations from the university's health and counseling services, the Office on Equity and Compliance, our disability resource center, and many more. What I learn in these meetings often informs my work in teaching and overseeing courses in NU Global. Not only do these visits better ensure that international students receive the support they need, but they also allow for cross-promotion because campus offices learn more about the ITC, as well.

Additional partnerships with campus offices demonstrate how the ITC helps internationalize Northeastern University. For example, the ITC works with the Office of Student Conduct and Conflict Resolution to offer special tutorials for international students who have been found to have violated the university's academic integrity policy. The ELS offers two hours of tutoring per week for international students at our Career Studio, as well. Over the years, various academic programs have also arranged to have a number of ITC appointments reserved for their students.

A particularly fruitful partnership is with the Northeastern Writing Center. In addition to meeting regularly to ensure that our policies continue to align, the ITC and the Writing Center have collaborated on several initiatives to not only promote our services but also provide general strategies for faculty to support multilingual writers. Initiatives have included a poster at a College of Professional Studies professional development conference, a "Meet the Tutors" event during International Education Week, and, with the Center for Advanced Teaching and Learning Through Research, the creation of instructional materials and four iterations of a workshop about providing feedback to multilingual writers. After attending one of these workshops, staff from a graduate program in the College of Engineering approached GSS and me to develop a course on communication skills and U.S. workplace acculturation. The course was launched in the spring of 2020 and is now offered regularly as an elective, thus providing more support for international students at Northeastern.

Challenges Faced by the ITC

Many of the features that have made the ITC popular among international students at Northeastern University have also contributed to its challenges, some of which we have been able to alleviate, while others persist.

Recruiting, Retaining, and Supervising Professional Tutors

Recruiting and retaining the professional tutors of the ITC is a persistent challenge. The hourly wage at the ITC is low given the qualifications required and Boston's high cost of living. As "temporary" employees, tutors are also not permitted to work more than 20 hours per week. Although tutors do accrue up to 40 hours of paid sick leave, they are not otherwise eligible for benefits. As a result, work at the ITC may be one of several jobs that a tutor juggles.

The impact of this labor arrangement on tutors is obvious and negative. At the administrative level, it limits who applies, complicates the schedule each semester, and prevents us from requiring that tutors attend staff meetings and retreats. This structure also means that, instead of fewer tutors working more hours, we tend to have *more* tutors working *fewer* hours. At one point, for example, the ITC employed 26 tutors. More tutors means more training, more evaluations, more timesheets, and generally more work for everyone involved.

We have attempted to mitigate this situation by creating as positive a workplace environment as possible, including actively seeking tutor input for all initiatives and paying them to participate in the staff meetings and other professional development opportunities we provide. The fact that 6 of the 12 current tutors have worked for the ITC for five years or more may be indicative of these efforts. Mostly, however, we recognize that the ITC may be an intermediary step in many tutors' careers and support them how we can (for example, inviting them to collaborate on presentations, serving as references, and writing letters of recommendation). Indeed, several ITC tutors have also gone on to secure full-time positions in other roles at NU Global, including the current ELS, who started as an ITC tutor.

Introducing the on-site ELS position was itself a challenge. The ITC is a 15-minute walk from GSS offices, and rarely are GSS staff or I present, which meant that tutors operated with a lot of independence. As experienced professionals, some tutors resented the implication that they suddenly required supervision. They also feared it would be awkward to conduct tutorials while someone was within earshot. To alleviate these concerns, the ITC space was configured so that the ELS sits in a reception area away from tutorials; likewise, we started playing soft, café-style music during tutorials.

What contributed most to tutors' acceptance of the ELS is that the ITC is undeniably a more professional and streamlined operation as a result of the efforts of the ELS. The ELS has assumed all administrative tasks once held by tutors, such as greeting students, checking them in, answering the phone, and keeping the ITC stocked and tidy. Due also to the diplomatic nature of the individual in this role, tutors now seem to recognize the value of this position. Each year, tutors are asked in their self-evaluations if they would like to acknowledge a colleague as having been especially helpful. In 2019 and 2020, the current ELS received the most praise.

Matching Students to Qualified Tutors

The fact that the ITC offers tutorials across such a wide range of skills makes it uniquely valuable, but this creates the challenge of matching each student with a tutor who has expertise in the skill the student would like to address. Ideally, a tutor is able to address all skills. However, it is more often the case that a tutor has expertise in some skills but not all. For example, a former speech pathologist may not feel comfortable offering instruction in citations. We have found that there is also less interest or experience among tutors toward some skills, particularly TOEFL® preparation. WCONLINE has a "limit to" function that students could use to find a tutor with expertise in the desired skill when making an appointment. Despite demonstrating this feature in class visits and videos about how to use the ITC, tutors still report that students make appointments regardless of tutor expertise. Simply put, students select appointments based mostly on their own availability, suggesting that additional tutor training across skills is the best solution.

Managing Student and Faculty Expectations of the ITC

In an internal investigation of ITC users' perceptions toward writing tutorials, I found that most students believed that the purpose of ITC tutorials was for tutors to find and correct all errors in student writing. In reality, when they visited the ITC, they encountered tutors who provided corrective feedback selectively. While this study confirmed that tutors were adhering to recommended practices, it indicated that tutors needed to better explain their approach; since then, this has been addressed in tutor trainings and information about corrective feedback was added to the website.

Similarly, a misperception held by some faculty is that it is the ITC's job and *not* theirs to foster the language development of international students. My colleagues and I believe that it is, in fact, a shared responsibility, but we also recognize that not everyone has expertise in second language teaching. Partnering with an ITC tutor, we created a poster presentation for a College of Professional Studies professional development conference to both promote the ITC and provide suggested practices specifically for supporting multilingual writers in the classroom (allowing drafts, explicitly teaching citation practices, etc.).

Unfortunately, it soon became clear that many attendees stopped reading after the ITC overview—"Oh, this is a great service! I'll just send my students there!"—and it seemed that we had only exacerbated the problem. The next year, we collaborated with the Northeastern Writing Center to create a similar poster, but, this time, we more explicitly explained the justification and theoretical background for our approach, as well as revised the poster's design to less prominently display the Writing Center and ITC information. We also added an announcement about our workshops on writing feedback, which seemed much more effective at conveying the message that if a teacher assigns writing, they must, to some extent, also teach it.

Access to Services

Of all challenges faced by the ITC, student access remains the most significant. Although we have dramatically increased the number of appointments offered, appointments often fill up two weeks in advance, which is the earliest students can register. Whereas students once joined the daily waiting list only at peak times (typically during the fall semester), there is now a waiting list year-round, once reaching as high as 150 students. Indeed, the most frequent suggestion from satisfaction surveys is to "Please offer more appointments."

Unfortunately, we face physical constraints preventing us from increasing the number of face-to-face appointments. To uphold a comfortable level of noise, only four tutorials are scheduled at one time at the main ITC. For the foreseeable future, it is also unlikely that additional branches will open because space is extremely limited at NU's urban campus, and the downtown branch proved to be less popular with students than the main ITC. Although online tutorials—which comprised all tutorials from March 2020 to the fall of 2021 as a result of the COVID-19 crisis—do not require physical space, the ITC is not a revenue-generating operation, so these too are limited by a finite budget. In the future, it may be necessary to seek grants or partner with other colleges or departments for increased funding. Until then, access remains our greatest challenge.

Implications

Prior to the 2020 pandemic, online appointments had always been among the last to fill, and an internal study in the spring of 2020 had found that students strongly preferred face-to-face tutorials. Since transitioning to online tutoring, however, our usage numbers have reached unprecedented highs, with between 88 to 93 percent of available appointments filled, and in the summer of 2020, we offered more appointments per week than any other previous summer. This further indicates that international students view the ITC as more than language support. It is a welcome, non-judgmental environment designed *just* for them. If they want to, they can make an appointment just to talk, and someone will listen. If they have a question, someone will answer. Even during a time of global anxiety and uncertainty, the ITC will be there to support them.

Some scholars (e.g., Cirillo-McCarthy et al., 2016) have described how (writing) centers exclusively serving international students can contribute to a deficit discourse. Hall (2013), however, acknowledged the advantages of a center staffed fully with ESL specialists, including the flexibility (and, I would argue, the knowledge) to provide more directive feedback if necessary, and resources specifically designed for international students. As a locus of expertise in the instruction of multilingual writing, the ITC is also poised to provide support for faculty across the disciplines. At the ITC, international students gain linguistic skills, awareness of academic culture, and, most importantly, the confidence to fully participate in classroom and campus activities. In this way, faculty concerns about language or cultural differences may be alleviated, and U.S. domestic students may benefit from more meaningful interactions with their international peers.

Despite the challenges, the ITC has been successful due to its comprehensive array of services, highly trained professional tutors, and promotional efforts that are often partnered with other university offices. We ensure quality by aligning our practices with second language scholarship and assessing them through internal research. As a result, the ITC is a unique and valued means of co-curricular support for the international students at Northeastern and may serve as a useful case study for other institutions as they strive to build their own models of comprehensive internationalization.

Acknowledgments

I wish to thank Whitney Wotkyns, Ethan Whittet, Annie Hsu, Patrick Plunkett, David Fields, Jeremy Rischall, and ITC tutors past and present for their work to support the success of international students at Northeastern University.

REFERENCES

Andrade, M. S., Evans, N. W., & Hartshorn, K. J. (2014). Linguistic support for non-native English speakers: Higher education practices in the United States. *Journal of Student Affairs Research and Practice, 51*(2), 207–221.

Babcock, R. D., & Thonus, T. (2018). *Researching the writing center: Towards an evidence-based practice* (Revised ed.). New York: Peter Lang.

Billedo, C. J., Kerkhof, P., & Finkenauer, C. (2020). More Facebook, less homesick? Investigating the short-term and long-term reciprocal relations of interactions, homesickness, and adjustment among international students. *International Journal of Intercultural Relations, 75*, 118–131.

Bruce, S., & Rafoth, B. A. (Eds.). (2009). *Tutoring ESL writers* (2nd ed.). Portsmouth, NH: Heinemann Boynton/Cook.

Cirillo-McCarthy, E., Del Russo, C., & Leahy, E. (2016). "We don't do that here": Calling out deficit discourses in the writing center to reframe multilingual graduate support. *Praxis: A Writing Center Journal, 14*(1). http://www.praxisuwc.com/cirillomccarty-141

Gautam, C., Lowery, C. L., Mays, C., & Durant, D. (2016). Challenges for global learners: A qualitative study of the concerns and difficulties of international students. *Journal of International Students, 6*(2), 501–526.

Hall, J. (2013). The impact of rising international student usage of writing centers. *Writing Lab Newsletter, 38*(1), 5–9.

Hegarty, N. (2014). Where we are now: The presence and importance to international students to universities in the United States. *Journal of International Students, 4*(3), 223–235.

Institute of International Education. (2020). *Leading host institutions.* Retrieved from https://opendoorsdata.org/data/international-students/leading-institutions/

Jin, L., & Schneider, J. (2019). Faculty views on international students: A survey study. *Journal of International Students, 9*(1) 84–96.

Jones, A. H., & Young, K. K. (2020). The role of academic self-confidence on thriving among international college students in the U.S. and Canada. *Journal of Underreported and Minority Progress, 4*(2), 165–191.

Knight, J. (2011). Five myths about internationalization. *International Higher Education, 62.* https://doi.org/10.6017/ihe.2011.62.8532

Kuo, Y. (2011). Language challenges faced by international graduate students in the United States. *Journal of International Students, 1*(2), 38–42.

Leask, B. (2015). *Internationalizing the Curriculum.* New York: Routledge.

Luo, J., & Jamieson-Drake, D. (2013). Examining the educational benefits of interacting with international students. *Journal of International Students, 3*(2), 85–101.

NAFSA (2020). *Economic tracking tool.* Retrieved from https://www.nafsa.org/policy-and-advocacy/policy-resources/nafsa-international-student-economic-value-tool-v2

Northeastern University (2016). *Academic Plan: Northeastern 2025.* Retrieved from https://www.northeastern.edu/academic-plan/plan/

Northeastern University. (2020a). *Global Student Success.* Retrieved from https://international.northeastern.edu/gss/

Northeastern University. (2020b). *International student hub.* Retrieved from https://international.northeastern.edu/

Özturgut, O., & Murphy, C. (2009). Literature vs. practice: Challenges for international students in the U.S. *International Journal of Teaching and Learning in Higher Education, 22*(3), 374–385.

Qureshi, F. H., & Khawaja, S. (2021). Is COVID-19 transitioning cash cows international students into cats? *European Journal of International Students, 8*(7), 204–219.

Trice, A. (2003). Faculty perceptions of graduate international students: The benefits and challenges. *Journal of Studies in International Education, 7*(4), 379–403.

3

Designing Virtual Learning Spaces to Promote Language and Cultural Exchange

D. Hannah Bush, Matthew Allen, Nancy Farner, and Nadezda Pimenova

Internationalization in higher education institutions (HEIs) encompasses a range of approaches for students' "development of intercultural understanding and skills for personal, professional, and citizenship development" (Knight, 2004, p. 22). International education programs provide numerous benefits at local and national levels (Altbach & Knight, 2007; Institute of International Education, 2019), and internationalization and internationalization-at-home (IaH) initiatives promote benefits for students who study and live in culturally diverse environments. Although English for Academic Purposes (EAP) programs have not historically framed their pedagogy in terms of IaH, EAP programs are well positioned to facilitate IaH outcomes because they are inherently attuned to the academic, language, and cultural needs of international students (Belcher, 2010).

Where IaH is an institutional goal, EAP programs must consider how to work toward that goal within their programs and with their students. One option is co-curricular collaborations or partner programs (see Rodríguez-Fuentes, Corrales, Paba, & Rosado-Mendinueta, this volume, and Ene & Cohen, this volume). However, it is often difficult to forge and sustain these types of partnerships, especially in today's dynamic higher education environments. Another option is for EAP programs to design learning spaces *inside* their courses so that students are better prepared for IaH opportunities *outside* of them. Like any academic unit, EAP programs may initially struggle to adapt because internationalization in the disciplines requires extensive work to transform curriculum and instruction (Leask, 2013).

One area where we have found success in incorporating IaH outcomes into our program is recognizing the need to prioritize virtual learning spaces that extend EAP coursework outside of the traditional classroom space. Thus, this chapter addresses ways that EAP programs can design virtual learning spaces to support both EAP and IaH outcomes. Drawing from instructional design models and the development of our EAP program, an approach to virtual learning spaces that engages learners in sustained, meaningful learning tasks to support the language and intercultural needs of EAP students and ultimately support IaH outcomes is described.

Context

Our EAP program is situated at Purdue University, a large research university in the U.S. Midwest with a long history of internationalization and a sizable population of international students (see Cheng, this volume). In 2019, international students from more than 100 nations comprised 13.8 percent of the total undergraduate student population, an increase of 65 percent over the previous ten years (Purdue University, 2019). Our EAP program—the Purdue Language and Cultural Exchange (PLaCE)—was created in 2014 in response to this increase of undergraduate international students at the university, with the mission of promoting advanced English language development and cultural competence among multilingual international students in a U.S. academic context. During this period of growth, Purdue also committed to transforming its pedagogy to more active, student-centered instruction and learning environments (Levesque-Bristol et al., 2019). This transformation means that academic, language, intercultural competencies of IaH initiatives all come into play, with students from different backgrounds regularly put into situations where they need to work together inside and outside of class.

To develop an EAP curriculum for this context, we identified three clusters of learning outcomes based on students' short- and long-term needs:

- **language and communication skills:** the cognitive and social language competencies that students develop and use in the university experience. Specific outcomes include vocabulary breadth and depth, speaking and listening proficiency, reading fluency and comprehension, and writing and presentation skills.

- **thinking and learning skills and strategies:** the social, linguistic, and cognitive abilities that university students need to develop to a high degree of expertise to succeed in their academic work in the 21st century (Kaufman, 2013; van Laar et al., 2017). These include self-regulated learning, collaboration, and group work; creative and critical thinking, reflection, source use, and citation practices; and media and technology literacy (Trilling & Fadel, 2009; Zimmerman, 1990).

- **intercultural knowledge and competence:** the "set of cognitive, affective, and behavior skills and characteristics that support effective and appropriate interaction in a variety of cultural contexts" (Bennett, 2008, p. 98). Specific outcomes include increased cultural self-awareness, attitudes of curiosity and openness to difference, appreciation of other perspectives and worldviews, and the ability to make comparisons and connections across diverse perspectives and experiences (Bennett, 2015; Deardorff, 2006).

We used these outcomes to design two courses (English 110 and English 111) for incoming international undergraduate students who score below our threshold on English language proficiency tests (currently set at 100 TOEFL® total score). English 110 and 111 are integrated skills courses that students take as a sequence over two semesters during their first year. The students are fully matriculated, which means they take the courses for academic credit while simultaneously taking courses in their majors.

This chapter focuses on English 110, which is organized into three sequential units implemented in a set of learning spaces: Unit 1 focuses on practical aspects of being a university student in the United States; Unit 2 explores intercultural learning experiences; and Unit 3 targets personal development and reflection. Course units and activities are integrated so that students learn through cycles of exploration, experience, observation, and reflection (Kolb, 2015).

Virtual Spaces as Sites for Meaningful, Authentic Learning

University life at an international campus is full of interesting spaces—academic, athletic, personal, cultural, social—and so the concept of *spaces* is often used to frame our pedagogy. We emphasize *learning spaces* with our students to explore how any space can become a site for learning. Ellis and Goodyear (2016) describe learning spaces as "different configurations and affordances of space designed, provided, supported, evaluated and renewed to enable learners to develop their understanding and skills" (p. 175). They note that any "'boundaries' between the physical and the virtual are becom[ing] less clear and more permeable" (p. 150). In a traditional model of higher education, learning spaces are tied to physical objects or places on campus (e.g., books, classrooms, libraries, or labs) and the transmission of knowledge. Many accepted assumptions and practices are being challenged, replaced, or transformed by increased use of digital tools and virtual instruction and modern pedagogies that view learning as an active and interactive process of inquiry and reflection, with learning tasks that are authentic and meaningful for students (Ellis & Goodyear, 2016).

Well-designed authentic tasks lead to meaningful learning experiences for students (Herrington, Reeves, & Oliver, 2014). Tasks are authentic when students work with real-world problems and solutions in learning environments that simulate or draw from real-world conditions (Lombardi, 2007). Other features of authentic learning tasks include:

○ problems with multiple possible solutions
○ sustained investigations that require students to collaborate and consider multiple perspectives
○ reflection by individuals and teams on their experience
○ assessment of student performance integrated into the learning process

Meaningful learning tasks are driven by "the pursuit of understanding through collaborative inquiry" and they "engage their students in the dialogue of knowledge building that aims for deeper understanding of the topics and issues studied" (Wells & Ball, 2008, p. 58). Meaningful learning in virtual spaces occurs when tasks extend beyond "testing inert knowledge" by facilitating opportunities for "students to learn how to recognize problems, comprehend new phenomena, construct mental models of those phenomena, and, given a new situation, set goals and regulate their own learning (learn how to learn)" (Jonassen et al., 2008, p. 2).

Our goal in designing our course to include virtual spaces was to create more authentic, meaningful intercultural and language interactions for students and instructors. At the curriculum level, we identified a core set of learning spaces for each course so that students in different sections have comparable ways to engage with course outcomes (e.g., units, projects). Within each learning space, instructors have room to create or adapt specific tasks for their courses. This mix of structure and flexibility allows instructors to adapt the curriculum to their strengths and their students' needs.

Designing Virtual Learning Spaces

Our approach to designing virtual learning spaces builds on the instructional design model ADDIE (analyze, design, develop, implement, evaluate), an iterative, systematic process that begins with a thorough needs analysis and subsequently aligns learning outcomes, objectives, assessments, and tasks to create effective, learner-centered environments (Branch & Merrill, 2012). Instructors need to account for many elements in the instructional design process, but we highlight six key elements here.

○ **Learning outcomes** are the knowledge, skills, attitudes, competencies, or habits of mind that students need to develop.

○ To achieve outcomes, instructors create **performance objectives**: descriptive statements of desired performance-based results by students, often put in terms of "can do" statements or in a template form ("students will be able to . . .") and followed by action verbs for observable behaviors (Krathwohl, 2002; Mager, 1962). These elements are determined by educators during an analysis of student and situational needs, and on the beliefs and judgments of the educators.

○ **Evaluation of learning** is considered throughout the instructional design process so that assessments can be embedded in the curriculum in ways that are coherent and equitable (Penuel & Shepard, 2016).

○ These initial choices are interpreted into a **virtual learning task** that ensures that teachers and students have a clear orientation point to bring everyone together and explain what students need to do, why, how, when, and with whom, and how they will be evaluated.

The final steps in the design process consist of choosing appropriate **digital genres** and **technology and tools**. Genres "provide a framework for interpreting and producing texts and for participating in mutually understood communicative acts"; additionally, digital genres have "unique features deriving from the multimodal, hypertextual and interactive affordances of the Internet" (Luzón, Ruiz-Madrid, & Villanueva, 2010 p. 9).

○ A **digital genre** is a flexible concept because genres are constantly evolving as creators regularly play with genre conventions as new technologies develop and old ones disappear (Davidson, 2010). Students develop their digital literacy as they figure out the conventions of various digital genres and try to situate their own work in relation to examples of a specific genre.

○ **Technologies and tools** are the specific apps, devices, platforms, or software programs. The key to choosing a specific tool or platform is to focus on "ways that technology can be used to bring out the very best in how teachers teach and how students learn" (Robin, 2008, p. 221). To design effective virtual spaces for learning of targeted outcomes, educators must consider how digital technologies will serve "as engagers and facilitators of thinking," language use, and interaction, and not merely "delivery vehicles" of content (Jonassen et al., 2008, p. 7).

Despite the potential of digital genres and technologies to create virtual learning spaces, it is problematic to assume that technologies are transparent or accessible to all students, or that digitally savvy students already know how to use familiar media and apps for educational purposes (Prensky, 2009). The notion of *spaces* is again helpful; students typically use digital technology for streaming videos in their entertainment spaces, while an EAP program's use of streaming video would be in language learning spaces. Prioritizing digital genres and technology tools without holistically assessing their affordances or limitations can distract from or even change the stated objectives (e.g., learning the technology for its own sake becomes the de facto learning goal). Non-systematic and inconsistent uses of technology in teaching can cause disconnects between the intended technology-enabled learning and students' actual experiences (Henderson, Selwyn, & Aston, 2017). Most of these challenges can be avoided or mitigated by intentionally working through the design process, starting with outcomes and objectives in mind.

Enacting the Design Process of Virtual Spaces

Two virtual learning spaces in English 110—video blogs and digital storytelling—are discussed to illustrate some specific tasks and digital technologies that instructors use within these spaces to enhance and even transform student learning.

Virtual Learning Space 1: Vlogs

From the outset, we recognized the need to address a recurring dilemma for our students. Our EAP students wanted to socialize with their peers and make friends with U.S.-born students while improving their academic English skills, yet struggled to do so because of the pressure to keep up with their other classes and commitments (such as family expectations and cultural groups from "back home"). As a result, students were often frustrated to find out that studying abroad was not the "ultimate opportunity to practice a foreign language" that they had imagined (DeKeyser, 2007, p. 208). To help address this situation, we added video blogs, or vlogs, to the English 110 curriculum. Vlogs provide a shared virtual learning space for students to connect with each other outside of class in the form of asynchronous videos posted to their course site. Because vlogs encourage students to work through course language and content with each other with limited interaction from the instructor, this virtual space encourages a "life-wide" perspective on course skills and content (Garrett & Barrett, 2009).

Outcomes, Objectives, and Evaluation

Vlog tasks leverage technology to help students develop their linguistic competency and the "cognitive and sociocultural skills necessary to gain access into the social, academic and workforce environments of the 21st century" (Ramachandran, 2004, p. 80). As with all learning spaces in the course, we try to balance academic, language, and cultural outcomes as we articulate performance objectives for students to demonstrate learning in this task:

1. **Language and communication skills:** Practice specific language and communication skills (e.g., fluent reading comprehension, pronunciation, hedging language, and discourse markers).

2. **Thinking and learning skills and strategies:** Work with classmates to analyze texts and personal experiences from different perspectives to develop thinking and learning skills and strategies.

3. **Intercultural knowledge and competence:** Reflect on their own and peers' perspectives about course concepts to develop intercultural awareness.

The primary evaluation in the vlog space is formative so that students have multiple chances for feedback and practice. Instructors are able to assess students' work on course objectives and provide personalized feedback to students or general feedback to a class. Additionally, vlogs create room for competency-based performance. Students can learn to measure their progress by reviewing their videos from the beginning of the course to the end. In this way, growth becomes "visible" to students.

Virtual Task

Instructors create vlog tasks to either prepare students for future class work or to push students to explore a topic further and engage in language practice after a class meeting. Vlogs are generally based on two kinds of tasks: **research-and-report** or **read-and-respond**. In the former, students do some informal, primary research on a topic from that week in class, so that they apply the course topics and language to their own life. In the latter, students read a text or watch a video with a transcript on a class topic. They then choose a short passage from the text or video transcript based on ideas that are particularly interesting, meaningful, or surprising to them. After deliberate practice, students record themselves reading this passage aloud and explain why they chose it. After recording their vlogs, students watch a classmate's video and respond.

Throughout the semester, instructors create prompts that reflect the unique interests and needs of their students as well as address a range of topics to foster students' development toward course outcomes. These types of vlog tasks push students to apply course content outside of class, build analytical skills as they find evidence to support their own and each other's ideas, and encourage students to spend time outside of class to reflect and refine their ideas. Vlogs provide a defined structure for students to work with while still affording them room to move around the virtual learning space to remake the course in their own words and perspectives.

Digital Genre, Technology, and Tools

We selected the genre of vlogs because it offers numerous affordances for instructors and students in technology-rich contexts. It crosses disciplines and formats and overlaps with other digital platforms, such as social media, that are already familiar to our students. Key genre features include documenting users' creative work (e.g., regular topical entries about their ideas and experiences) and interactive work (i.e., users actively watch and respond to each other). Working within this genre promotes a learning community among students through a balance of social interaction, language learning, and higher order thinking (Huang & Hung, 2013).

To implement vlogs as effective virtual learning spaces, instructors need to select tools based on relevant criteria such as accessibility, interactivity, and usability. Apps and platforms that simulate real-world conditions facilitate more authentic learning tasks. The virtual and real worlds are more integrated when tools are more accessible for students to work on multiple platforms in many countries. Cloud-based platforms such as Flipgrid (https://info.flipgrid.com/) have worked well for us because they meet these criteria and reflect many familiar social media interactions in which students have online discussions by posting and responding to each other in short videos (Green & Green, 2018).

Virtual Learning Space 2: Digital Storytelling

For the final project of our course, we designed a virtual learning space for digital storytelling based on personal reflection. Throughout the development of the course, we have regularly drawn from personal stories and reflections to help students work toward language and intercultural outcomes. Media we use includes TED Talks such as "The Danger of a Single Story" by Chimamanda Ngozi Adichie, "Don't Ask Where I'm from, Ask Where I'm a Local" by Taiye Selasi, and "How to Find a Wonderful Idea" by the band OK Go. These storytellers interpret, and often re-interpret, their personal experiences to challenge accepted norms, upset stereotypes, and push back at labels assigned to them.

Such stories from the media resonated with our students because they openly discuss how individuals navigate their identities across languages and cultures. We were also inspired by the stories our students told us in class, in vlogs, and during office hours about how they were navigating their diverse (and often conflicting) spaces during this transformational time in their life. Their stories challenged our assumptions about our students and their international educational experiences, and they changed how we saw our students by helping us to see the university from their eyes. As a result, our final project evolved from traditional in-class presentations on course topics to reflective storytelling projects.

Outcomes, Objectives, and Evaluation

Within the digital storytelling space at the end of the course, instructors design a specific task for each student to create a recorded presentation of an original, reflective digital story. As with all learning spaces in the course, we try to balance outcomes as we articulate performance objectives for students to demonstrate learning in this project:

1. **language and communication skills:** Use listener-friendly speech to present their ideas in a focused, organized, and well-developed narrative.

2. **thinking and learning skills and strategies:** Evaluate their personal development and experiences at the university in relation to course concepts (e.g., time management), models (e.g., comfort zones), and tools.

3. **intercultural knowledge and competence:** Reflect on their trajectory of self-awareness, openness and appreciation of difference, and ability to compare and contrast across diverse experiences.

Reflection and storytelling are closely related, and we view reflective storytelling as an intentional, authentic process of knowledge creation and sharing (Herrington et al., 2014; Merrill, 2002). Like any form of interpretation, personal reflection is a process of telling stories based on evidence and reason. Reflection as storytelling is a form of sophisticated thinking about oneself combined with the challenge of communicating that knowledge of self to others. The extension to digital storytelling is both practical and theoretical: incorporating digital media into one's story literally and figuratively helps others see another person's point of view. Thus, reflective digital storytelling becomes a potent space for language, academic, and intercultural learning.

Students are graded on the quality of their digital story presentation in terms of project objectives and requirements. We do not assess the quality of students' experiences as college students. Instructors assess how effectively students demonstrate reflective thinking, integrate course vocabulary and concepts, address issues of cultural adjustment, and demonstrate personally meaningful development. Instructors also evaluate students' academic presentation skills. Because it is an assignment for an EAP course, students need to meet appropriate standards for academic communication in terms of language use, clarity, and structure of ideas.

Virtual Task

The goal of this project is for students to reflect on their experiences and create an original narrative in the form of a digital story that uses themes, terms, and concepts from the class to show how they have developed over the course of the semester. Students are required to create a video that tells a meaningful story connecting course concepts to their academic, cultural, language, personal, and/or social development. Students often start with active situations or problems in their lives (such as learning to be independent, dealing with new responsibilities, and adapting to new cultural expectations and norms) and create their digital stories through several rounds of drafting and instructor and peer feedback.

Digital Genre, Technology, and Tools

Digital storytelling is a broad genre, and there are many resources to orient students (such as the site Educational Uses of Digital Storytelling https://digitalstorytelling.coe.uh.edu, maintained by Bernard Robin at the University of Houston). Digital technologies play an important role in the genre, as Robin (2008) explains:

> At its core, digital storytelling allows computer users to become creative storytellers through the traditional processes of selecting a topic, conducting some research, writing a script, and developing an interesting story. This material is then combined with various types of multimedia, including computer-based graphics, recorded audio, computer-generated text, video clips, and music [so that it can be shared digitally]. (p. 222)

When successfully integrated into a task, digital tools support students' reflection by increasing engagement with learning and with peers (Rose, Sierschynski, & Bjorling, 2016; Sadik, 2008). Language is an essential part of reflection, intercultural competence, and digital storytelling, so instructors and students must account for language learning and use and look for ways to use digital storytelling to improve students' English proficiency (Chung & Yunus, 2018; Galante, 2014). Robin (2008) describes the type of digital storytelling that we do as "personal narratives." This label aligns with the idea of sharing one's personal connections and contributions to a community and fits with research showing that digital storytelling practices can help multilingual students navigate their learning experiences and their identities (Vinogradova, 2011).

One of our favorite digital formats for this project is a PechaKucha presentation because it provides a clear structure to work with (a slideshow of 20 slides that show for 20 seconds each, with each slide using simple images and minimal text) while still providing room for individuals to create projects that achieve course objectives for language use, application of course concepts, and personal reflection. PechaKucha presentations also connect students to a global community: the presentation format was created in Japan but has spread globally through local events and the organization's website (www.pechakucha.com).

Lessons Learned about Virtual Learning Spaces

Learning spaces is a simple concept that has resonated with our students and instructors and has proved to be remarkably robust in helping us to implement our curriculum and meet students' learning needs as our program has transitioned to operating in virtual learning spaces in unexpected ways.

When designing for any learning space, we are continually reminded to follow the instructional design maxim to "start with the end in mind" (with that end being students' achievement of learning outcomes and program goals of internationalization on our campus). Within and across learning spaces, instructors need to design appropriately complex tasks and appropriate support that "help learners to integrate the knowledge, skills, and attitudes necessary for effective task performance; give them the opportunity to learn to coordinate constituent skills that make up complex task performance; and eventually enable them to transfer what they learned to their daily life or work settings" (van Merriënboer et al., 2003, p. 5). Importantly, technologies should *enhance* the learning process, not *drive* the instructional design process. In a language program, digital tools and platforms are facilitators for instructors and students, not the starting point or end goal.

Building effective virtual learning spaces requires intentional scaffolding of meaningful concepts and tasks. Scaffolding is an appropriate analogy here because of its imagery of instructors who guide students to construct their own independent learning. Learning spaces are building sites, and while an effective curriculum provides a blueprint, it is the instructors and students who do the work of learning, with students taking on progressively more complex tasks with decreasing support and increasing responsibility (Fisher & Frey, 2013; Wood, Bruner, & Ross, 1976). Likewise, genres provide students and instructors room to explore but also boundaries to guide their learning. Everyone benefits when meaningful learning spaces are structured so that individuals feel connected to others but still have enough autonomy to develop their own competencies (Niemiec & Ryan, 2009). Scaffolded support need not be restricted to individual courses. Support structures for transfer can also be bridges that extend virtual learning spaces across EAP courses and connect EAP students with other units on campus. For example, we have extended our virtual learning spaces for vlogs and digital storytelling from English 110 into English 111, the second course in our sequence, as part of a digital portfolio (which is another virtual learning space in which students collect their best work across their two-semester course sequence in our program).

Another important lesson for us is that the instructional design process is never really finished; rather, it is an iterative process of building and rebuilding learning spaces. In 2020 (the year of the global pandemic), these lessons were especially vivid, as our program pivoted from traditional operations (on-campus, in-person instruction) to operating almost entirely online with students in their home countries. This sudden transition evolved from having a few virtual learning spaces in every course to operating almost exclusively in virtual learning spaces. Our design process has been resilient in the face of changing educational contexts, and it has helped us to transform our practice as we transition between traditional and virtual tasks. Regardless of factors beyond our control such as the global COVID-19 pandemic, we have been encouraged to see that these virtual learning spaces can help to change our students' understanding of themselves and their classmates. We believe that their stories can change others' preconceived notions and expectations about what it means to be an international student. The real measure of success of this design process is whether students can transform their work with us to build their own learning spaces for language and cultural exchanges. Although this approach to instructional design inside an EAP course is not sufficient for internationalization, it does important work toward that end by creating spaces for students to develop their academic, language, and intercultural competencies.

REFERENCES

Altbach, P. G., & Knight, J. (2007). The internationalization of higher education: Motivations and realities. *Journal of Studies in International Education, 11*(3–4), 290–305. https://doi.org/10.1177/1028315307303542

Belcher, D. (2010). What ESP is and can be: An introduction. In D. Belcher (Ed.), *English for specific purposes in theory and practice* (pp. 1–20). Ann Arbor: University of Michigan Press.

Bennett, J. M. (2008). Transformative training: Designing programs for culture learning. In M. A. Moodian (Ed.), *Contemporary leadership and intercultural competence: Understanding and utilizing cultural diversity to build successful organizations* (pp. 95–110). Thousand Oaks, CA: Sage.

Bennett, J. M. (2015). *The Sage encyclopedia of intercultural competence.* Thousand Oaks, CA: Sage.

Branch, R. M., & Merrill, M. D. (2012). Characteristics of instructional design models. In R. A. Reiser and J. V. Dempsey (Eds.), *Trends and issues in instructional design and technology* (pp. 8–16). Boston: Pearson.

Chung, J., & Yunus, M. M. (2018). Digital storytelling production as a learning tool in improving ESL learners' verbal proficiency. *The Asian EFL Journal, 20*(5), 131–141. Retrieved May 31, 2020 from https://www.asian-efl-journal.com/monthly-editions -new/2018-teaching-articles/volume-20-issue-5-2018/#squelch-taas-tab-content-0-1

Davidson, D. (2010). *Cross-media communications: An introduction to the art of creating integrated media experiences.* Pittsburgh: Carnegie Mellon University Press. https://doi. org/10.1184/R1/6686735

Deardorff, D. K. (2006). Identification and assessment of intercultural competence as a student outcome of internationalization. *Journal of Studies in International Education, 10*(3), 241–266. https://doi.org/10.1177/1028315306287002

DeKeyser, R. M. (2007). Study abroad as foreign language practice. In R. M. DeKeyser (Ed.), *Practice in a second language: Perspectives from applied linguistics and cognitive psychology* (pp. 208–226). New York: Cambridge University Press.

Ellis, R. A., & Goodyear, P. (2016). Models of learning space: Integrating research on space, place and learning in higher education. *Review of Education, 4*(2), 149–191. https://doi.org/10.1002/rev3.3056

Fisher, D., & Frey, N. (2013). *Better learning through structured teaching: A framework for the gradual release of responsibility* (2nd ed.). Alexandria, VA: ASCD.

Galante, A. (2014). Developing EAL learners' intercultural sensitivity through a digital literacy project. *TESL Canada Journal, 32*(1), 53–53. https://doi.org/10.18806/tesl.v32i1.1199

Garrett, N., & Barrett, H. C. (2009). Online personal learning environments: Structuring electronic portfolios for lifelong and life wide learning. *On the Horizon, 17*(2), 142–152. https://doi.org/10.1108/10748120910965511

Green, T., & Green, J. (2018). Flipgrid: Adding voice and video to online discussions. *TechTrends, 62*(1), 128–130. https://doi.org/10.1007/s11528-017-0241-x

Henderson, M., Selwyn, N., & Aston, R. (2017). What works and why? Student perceptions of 'useful' digital technology in university teaching and learning. *Studies in Higher Education, 42*(8), 1567–1579. https://doi.org/10.1080/03075079.2015.1007946

Herrington, J., Reeves, T. C., & Oliver, R. (2014). Authentic learning environments. In Spector, J., Merrill, M., & Bishop, M. (Eds.), *Handbook of research on educational communications and technology* (pp. 401–412). New York: Springer. https://doi.org/10.1007/978-1-4614-3185-5_32

Huang, H-T. D., & Hung, S-T. A. (2013). Exploring the utility of a video-based online EFL discussion forum. *British Journal of Educational Technology, 44*(3), E90–E94. https://doi.org/10.1111/j.1467-8535.2012.01373.x

Institute of International Education. (2019). *Open doors report on international educational exchange.* Institute of International Education. Retrieved August 28, 2020 from https://opendoorsdata.org/annual-release/

Jonassen, D. H., Howland, J. L, Marra, R. M., & Crismond, D. P. (2008). *Meaningful learning with technology* (3rd ed.). Upper Saddle River, NJ: Pearson Education.

Kaufman, K. J. (2013). 21 ways to 21st century skills: Why students need them and ideas for practical implementation. *Kappa Delta Pi Record, 49*(2), 78–83. https://doi.org/10.1080/00228958.2013.786594

Knight, J. (2004). Internationalization remodeled: Definition, approaches, and rationales. *Journal of Studies in International Education, 8*(1), 5–31. https://doi.org/10.1177/1028315303260832

Kolb, D. A. (2015). *Experiential learning: Experience as the source of learning and development.* Upper Saddle River, NJ: Pearson Education.

Krathwohl, D. R. (2002). A revision of Bloom's taxonomy: An overview. *Theory into Practice, 41*(4), 212–218. https://doi.org/10.1207/s15430421tip4104_2

Leask, B. (2013). Internationalizing the curriculum in the disciplines—Imagining new possibilities. *Journal of Studies in International Education, 17*(2), 103–118. https://doi.org/10.1177/1028315312475090

Levesque-Bristol, C., Flierl, M., Zywicki, C., Parker, L. C., Connor, C. Guberman, C., Nelson, D., Maybee, C, Bonem, E., FitzSimmons, J., & Lott, E. (2019). *Creating student-centered learning environments and changing teaching culture: Purdue University's IMPACT program. Occasional Paper #38*. Urbana: University of Illinois and Indiana University, National Institute for Learning Outcomes Assessment. Retrieved August 29, 2020 from https://eric.ed.gov/?id=ED594392

Lombardi, M. M. (2007). Authentic learning for the 21st century: An overview. *Educause Learning Initiative*, 1–12. Retrieved December 2, 2018 https://library.educause.edu/resources/2007/1/authentic-learning-for-the-21st-century-an-overview

Luzón, M. J., Ruiz-Madrid, M. N., & Villanueva, M. L. (2010). Learner autonomy in digital environments: Conceptual framework. In M. J. Luzón, M. N. Ruiz-Madrid, & M. L. Villanueva (Eds.). *Digital genres, new literacies and autonomy in language learning* (pp. 1–24). Newcastle-upon-Tyne, England: Cambridge Scholars Publishing.

Mager, R. F. (1962). *Preparing instructional objectives*. Palo Alto, CA: Fearon.

Merrill, M. D. (2002). First principles of instruction. *Educational Technology Research & Development, 50*(3), 43–59. https://doi.org/10.1007/BF02505024

Niemiec, C. P., & Ryan. R. (2009). Autonomy, competence, and relatedness in the classroom: Applying self-determination theory to educational practice. *Theory and Research in Education, 7*(2),133–144. https://doi.org/10.1177/1477878509104318

Penuel, W. R., & Shepard, L. (2016). Assessment and teaching. In D.H. Gitomer & C.A. Bell (Eds.)., *Handbook of research on teaching* (5th ed., pp. 787–850). American Educational Research Association. https://doi.org/10.3102/978-0-935302-48-6_12

Prensky, M. (2009). H. sapiens digital: From digital immigrants and digital natives to digital wisdom. *Innovate: Journal of Online Education, 5*(3). Retrieved May 30, 2019 from https://www.learntechlib.org/p/104264/

Purdue University. (2019). *International students and scholars enrollment and statistical report*. West Lafayette, IN. Retrieved August 30, 2020 from https://www.purdue.edu/IPPU/ISS/reports.html

Ramachandran, S. (2004). Integrating new technologies into language teaching: Two activities for an EAP classroom. *TESL Canada Journal, 22*(1), 79–90. https://doi.org/10.18806/tesl.v22i1.167

Robin, B. R. (2008). Digital storytelling: A powerful technology tool for the 21st Century classroom. *Theory into Practice, 47*(3), 220–228. https://doi.org/10.1080/00405840 802153916

Rose, E., Sierschynski, J., & Bjorling, E. (2016). Reflecting on reflections: Using video in learning reflection to enhance authenticity. *The Journal of Interactive Technology and Pedagogy.* Retrieved May 31, 2020 from https://jitp.commons.gc.cuny.edu/reflecting-on-reflections-using-video-in-learning-reflection-to-enhance-authenticity/

Sadik, A. (2008). Digital storytelling: A meaningful technology-integrated approach for engaged student learning. *Educational Technology Research and Development, 56,* 487–506. https://doi.org/10.1007/s11423-008-9091-8

Trilling, B., & Fadel, C. (2009). *21st century skills: Learning for life in our times.* San Francisco: Jossey-Bass.

van Laar, E., van Deursen, A. J. A. M., van Dijk, J. A. G. M., & de Haan, J. (2017). The relation between 21st-century skills and digital skills: A systematic literature review. *Computers in Human Behavior, 72,* 577–588. https://doi.org/10.1016/j.chb.2017.03.010

van Merriënboer, J. J. G., Kirschner, P. A., & Kester, L. (2003). Taking the load off a learner's mind: Instructional design for complex learning. *Educational Psychologist, 38*(1), 5–13. https://doi.org/10.1207/S15326985EP3801_2

Vinogradova, P. (2011). *Digital storytelling in ESL instruction: Identity negotiation through a pedagogy of multiliteracies.* Unpublished doctoral diss., University of Maryland, Baltimore County.

Wells, G., & Ball, T. (2008). Understanding: The purpose of education. In C. Nygaard & C. Holtham (Eds.), *Understanding learning-centered higher education* (pp. 51–75). Copenhagen: Copenhagen Business School Press.

Wood, D., Bruner, J. S., & Ross, G. (1976). The role of tutoring in problem solving. *Journal of Child Psychology and Psychiatry, 17*(2), 89–100. https://doi.org/10.1111/j.1469-7610.1976.tb00381.x

Zimmerman, B. J. (1990). Self-regulated learning and academic achievement: An overview. *Educational Psychologist, 25*(1), 3–17. https://doi.org/10.1207/s15326985ep2501_2

4

Promoting Communicative and Intercultural Competence Development through Virtual Exchanges

Rodrigo A. Rodríguez-Fuentes, Kathleen A. Corrales, Lourdes Rey Paba, and Nayibe Rosado-Mendinueta

The internationalization of higher education has foregrounded the need for language programs to prepare students to communicate across cultures. The general purpose of internationalization in the language classroom is to catalyze the development of intercultural communicative competence, which is understood as the ability to interact effectively with people from another country and culture, not only in their own language but also in a foreign language (Byram, 1997; López-Rocha, 2016). Figuring out how to provide students with opportunities to develop these skills is an important and timely challenge for language programs and can be an important part of internationalization-at-home (IaH) initiatives, which ultimately seek to integrate the international and intercultural dimensions into the curriculum (formally and informally) of all students in domestic learning environments (Beelen & Jones, 2015).

In some contexts, such as campuses with many international or study abroad students, this outcome may be achieved by means of language exchanges or adapted curricula (see Bush, Allen, Farner,

79

& Pimenova, this volume, and Cheng, this volume). However, most higher educational institutions worldwide serve primarily domestic students, of which only a minority will engage in study abroad or interact with students from other countries. Even foreign language classrooms and study abroad experiences often lack opportunities for students to use the target language outside the classroom. Consequently, instructors need to provide students with experiences to engage in authentic intercultural interactions, often through tasks that make use of technological opportunities.

One version of IaH that rose in popularity in schools and colleges around the world in the 1980s was pen pal letter exchanges, in which students were paired with other students to carry out tasks. The extent and scope of the pen pal friendships ranged from improving literacy skills in one's first language (L1) (Baker & Brown, 1984; Wells, 1996) and encouraging collaborative projects in math and science (Lemkuhl, 2002) to practicing foreign language skills and supporting intercultural awareness with people in different parts of the world (Barksdale, Watson, & Park, 2007).

With the advent of the World Wide Web in the 1990s, digital versions of pen pal programs started to emerge as an alternative in contexts with those capabilities. In the case of language teaching, virtual exchanges (VEs) arose and, even today, are an opportunity to interact with target language users and explore intercultural endeavors. During most of the 21st century and due to technology and institutional agreements, different versions of VEs are used around the world to create practical, inclusive, meaningful, and solidarity experiences in foreign language learning.

Issues and Challenges That Motivated Our Research

Traditionally, providing foreign language students with opportunities to interact meaningfully with others in the target language has been a challenge for teachers, as well as for schools and college officials, due to the costs and logistics of moving students physically around the world.

With rare exceptions, study abroad initiatives are expensive, time con-suming, and create issues with equity because typically only a small por-tion of the student population can participate in exchanges. The result is that only those universities with more individual, institutional, or national resources are able to send students abroad. Other challenges to mobility opportunities that create further concerns about international travel include political, economic, or public health crises in any of the countries involved (such as during the COVID-19 pandemic).

Due to the widespread access to the internet during the first part of the 21st century, students in foreign language classes have benefited from digital forms of interaction with foreign audiences, such as blogs and chat rooms, but also from virtual exchanges. For this study, VEs can be defined as "the engagement of groups of learners in online inter-cultural interactions and collaboration projects with partners from other cultural contexts or geographical locations as an integrated part of their educational programmes" (O'Dowd, 2018, p. 1). Since the late 1990s, this concept has been described using a variety of terms in the fields of applied linguistics and foreign language education: telecollabo-ration, online intercultural exchange, virtual exchange, collaborative online international learning, internet-mediated intercultural foreign language education, globally networked learning environments, and e-tandem or teletandem language exchange (O'Dowd, 2017, 2018). No matter the term used, the benefits of implementing VEs are that stu-dents can develop both their language as well as their intercultural com-petences while interacting with students in other places in the world (Belz, 2003).

Despite the fact that VE is a relatively new pedagogical practice, researchers have quickly built a strong body of literature on its impact in teaching and learning (Helm, 2019; O'Dowd, 2017, 2018; O'Dowd & Lewis, 2016). Gläsman (2004) emphasized that using VEs helps learn-ers to interact with real people in real time, allowing students to per-ceive their growth in language accuracy and fluency (Kötter, 2003; Lee, 2006; Tian & Wang, 2010) and intercultural communicative compe-tence (Belz, 2007; García, Rey, & Rosado, 2010, 2009; Möllering & Levy, 2012). Other studies have found virtual exchanges to be dynamic (Pel-lettieri, 2000), interactive (Schenker, 2017), and motivating for students

(Yamada, 2009). There is strong evidence that suggests that VEs also promote learner autonomy (Fuchs, Hauck, & Müller-Hartmann, 2012; O'Rourke, 2005) and teachers' and students' positive attitudes toward autonomous language learning (Helm, 2015).

Context of the Curricular Innovation

This innovation took place at the Universidad del Norte (Uninorte), a large private, non-profit university located in the north of Colombia. More than 99 percent of its 16,000 students are Colombian, but IaH efforts have become stronger over the last few years (García, Rey, & Rosado, 2010, 2009; Mizuno et al., 2006; Rey & Rosado, 2001). The low rate of international students on campus, along with budget constraints that limit massive study abroad programs, are two of the strongest motivations for promoting VEs. These exchanges also have helped to define the professional profile of our students as citizens of the world and interculturally literate individuals who are capable of interacting across professional contexts. Functional proficiency in English is the first goal, followed by intercultural awareness. The combination of these two factors—language use and competent interaction—frame the development of intercultural communicative competencies in language learners while creating meaningful academic ties with peers in other universities.

The VE presented in this study took place in the highest level (out of eight) of a general undergraduate English program. In this course, students approach their language learning using themes related to aspects of intercultural communication such as culture (definition of culture and main aspects; religion; stereotypes; and models of categorization of cultures), subcultures (discrimination of subcultures by race, religion, and gender), and verbal and non-verbal intercultural communication. The Colombian students interacted with peers from the United States who were learning Spanish. In general, the Colombian students had a high-intermediate level of the language while the U.S. students had a low-intermediate level. Similar to other VE experiences (see O'Rourke, 2005), students provided feedback to their peers to enhance awareness of how language is learned and used. Professors provided examples and practice in class to model giving feedback clearly and respectfully. This included guiding students to provide feedback on both the written and oral work of their peers by identifying common errors in grammar and vocabulary use. Thus, in this experience, the role of professors was focused on facilitating the exchange and setting house rules. They assigned partners, co-designed activities with their counterparts abroad, and ensured that students were completing their assignments.

The VE was designed so that students from two different cultural and linguistic backgrounds had opportunities to communicate. The aim for the eight-week exchange was for students to learn each other's languages (Spanish and English) and also learn about each other's cultures (Colombian and U.S.). Communication among students was typically half in English and half in Spanish, allowing participants equitable opportunities to practice in the language they were studying with authentic input.

As part of the VE, students were given a pool of activities, topics, and platforms that they could use. For example, in terms of activities, students could either create a video or write a letter to introduce themselves and their culture. As for the topics of the course, students could select aspects related to culture that they wanted to explore with their assigned partners (e.g., religion, celebrations, family and cultural values, notions of beauty, etc.). Students also could interact synchronously or asynchronously with their partners using the platform that was available to both (Skype, Blackboard Collaborate, WhatsApp, Facetime, Zoom). For example, WhatsApp is a very popular app among Colombian students while it is not as well-known by students in the United States; as a result, the students had to negotiate which communication platform to use.

Overview of Virtual Exchange Structure

As mentioned earlier, the main goal of the VE was to allow students the opportunity to interact and grow in both their language skills and intercultural competence. Therefore, the intercultural communicative competencies that were the focus of the VE were knowledge of and openness to other cultures. Part of this includes learning about the other culture's customs, beliefs, and values while at the same time reevaluating the validity of stereotypes held about the other culture.

The learning outcomes were to compare and contrast aspects of one's own and the other's cultures and then express those ideas in a discussion (extemporaneously). For the VE, students from Colombia were paired with students from the United States in all activities. The four activities that made up the VE were:

○ Activity 1: "Who Am I and Who Are You?" Letter or Video: Before this activity, professors of the two institutions decided which group would begin the VE. In class, those students created one video or wrote one letter in which they introduced themselves. Students were instructed to provide information about themselves (interests, studies, family, etc.) and a brief description of their country and city in the video/letter. Students were also tasked with asking questions to their VE partner (e.g., What do you do in your free time? Why are you studying Spanish/English? What is life like in your country?). After receiving their partner's video or letter, the VE partner created and sent their own video/letter following the guidelines above and responded to their partner's questions. Students were given one week to complete this activity.

○ Activity 2: Video Chats: After completing Activity 1, students were expected to hold at least two formal video chats with their corresponding VE peer once every two weeks for a minimum of 15 minutes, half in Spanish and half in English. During these video chats, students were instructed to talk about aspects of their lives they wanted to explore more or to discuss aspects of the two cultures to identify similarities and differences. Partners were also encouraged to provide each other with feedback on language (pronunciation, grammar, vocabulary). Students were instructed to record these encounters using the tools available in the different platforms as evidence of completion of the work. Many students extended these encounters for longer than required (e.g., 40 minutes, one hour). Some students also had more interactive sessions than required for the class.

○ Activity 3: Collaborative Compare/Contrast Essay about College Life: Each student had to research the life of college students in the other culture (U.S. students learned about Colombia and Colombian students learned about the United States). To obtain information, students also wrote a series of questions (e.g., Do students usually work while they study? Is the curriculum flexible? Do students live in dorms?) that they asked their language partner through a video chat. Each student then composed the essay and sent it via email to their partner for language feedback. Teachers were copied on the email to ensure that each student wrote their essay in the target language. Students were given two weeks to complete this assignment.

○ Activity 4: Presentation about Partner and Partner's Culture (Evaluation): After completing the VE activities with their partner, Uninorte students prepared a presentation for their class in which they described their partner and details about their culture, including comparisons and contrasts with the Colombian culture. Finally, they concluded with a reflection about what they learned during the project in terms of culture and language.

Our Research Question and Methods

To assess the gains of the Colombian students, we considered student perspectives as to how VEs relate to the development of communicative and intercultural competences. The guiding question for our research was: What are the students' perceptions of their own intercultural communicative competence after participating in a VE experience?

This study used sequential explanatory design (Creswell, 2003, 2014). In the first phase, we gathered data on students' perceptions of their communicative and intercultural competence through pre- and post-surveys and processed this data using statistical procedures. In the second phase, we collected qualitative data from student reflections and then did a content analysis to aid the interpretation of the statistical results.

Participants

The participants in the VE were undergraduate students from two different universities, one located in the United States and one in Colombia. The students were from a variety of majors and were completing their foreign language requirement at their respective institutions. The data from the study presented here were gathered in the fall 2018 and spring 2019 terms. The U.S. students were from a university located on the east coast of the United States, while the Colombians were all from Uninorte in Barranquilla. We report the data *only* from the 36 official participants on the Colombian side of the exchange.

Instruments

The survey used to collect student perceptions on intercultural topics contained 18 statements that elicited a response on a 4-point Likert-type scale (1=strongly disagree, 2=disagree, 3=agree, 4=strongly agree), which are presented in Appendix 4A. The survey was originally created by Cano and Ricardo (2014) as part of their doctoral dissertation and has been adapted and adopted by Universidad del Norte as the institutional tool to measure intercultural development. The competencies in the survey focus on student awareness of their own values and prejudices, their cultural perspectives, and culturally appropriate practices they use when interacting.

Data collection for the survey and reflections were carried out following Cohen, Manion, and Morrison (2011) and Denzin and Lincoln (2018), who describe procedures under pre- and post-conditions. The survey was applied before the VE and again after the eight-week experience to determine if there were changes on the self-perceptions of cultural competence.

Students completed a semi-structured reflection in which we asked them to complete some statements about the virtual experience: *(1) From this experience, I learned . . .; (2) Some of the challenges I faced were . . .; (3) I faced these challenges by . . .; (4) When interacting with people from other cultures, I realized. . . .* The responses were then analyzed to triangulate the information from the surveys.

Survey and Reflection Analysis

Due to its ordinal nature, the Likert-type scale yields categorical data. Only non-parametric statistics were used to analyze these data. A Wilcoxon test was applied to statistically identify changes on the students' responses between the pre- and post-survey.

For the reflections on VE elicited at the end of the experience, the researchers employed content analysis (Elo et al., 2014). Coding was used to classify recurrent themes in the reflections. To build intercoder reliability, each researcher analyzed individually a small portion of the reflections; later, the emerging categories were discussed, and the final codes were agreed upon. Randomly selected samples equivalent to 15 percent of the total number of reflections were assigned to all coders. These samples were checked for intercoding accuracy and had an agreement of 91 percent.

Results and Discussion

Pre-/Post-Survey Analysis

The analysis of the results yielded statistically significant differences before and after the VE. Positive changes, as measured by stronger agreement with the statements, were observed in 10 out of 19 abilities included in the survey. From the survey analysis, the significantly different statements were grouped into three main categories that included general intercultural competences: (1) *knowing the other*, which refers to what the students learned from the other culture; (2) *knowing myself*, which relates to learning about themselves in relation to the other; and (3) *interacting with the other*, which can be associated with the interplay between the student and their partner. Competencies related to interactions with others changed the most, since there were five statements that showed positive effects. These were:

○ identify attitudes, beliefs, and values that show respect and appreciation toward other cultures (Statement 5)

○ describe a situation in which a person has offended someone because of racism, prejudice, discrimination, and stereotypes (S11)

○ identify behaviors that cause discrimination (S13)

○ establish dialogues about differences in beliefs based on culture (S14)

○ recognize how emotional reactions of other groups influence behavior (S18)

These findings fulfill the expectations of the experience because one of the objectives of the VE was for students to grow, along with their peer(s), in intercultural competence, which includes topics related to their cultural values and beliefs, including educated opinions on stereotypes.

The second category that showed a positive change was the one related to students knowing their own culture and themselves. These aspects were:

○ identifying the attitudes, beliefs and values that prevent them from respecting or appreciating other cultures (Statement 6)

○ recognizing their own cultural heritage and identifying its characteristics (S8 and S9)

○ recognizing their own stereotypes toward different cultures (S16)

Activities were designed to encourage thought on both the students' own culture and ideas as well as those of their partners.

The third topic that was significantly affected by the VE is related to knowledge about the attitudes and beliefs of the other cultures (S2). Again, learning about their partner's culture was one of the main focuses of the experience; therefore, this change is not surprising. These results provide consistent evidence that the VE had positive effects on three main areas of intercultural competencies. This finding adds to the body of evidence from previous studies of programs that used VEs (Belz, 2007; García, Rey, & Rosado, 2009, 2010; Mizuno et al., 2006; Möllering & Levy, 2012; Rey & Rosado, 2001). In general, the competencies that showed positive changes were closely related to the activities developed in the VE that allowed students to recognize their own cultural traits and compare them with those of their partners.

Reflections Analysis

In general, findings from the reflections demonstrated that students felt that they benefited from the experience in terms of language and intercultural competence development. One of the biggest gains for students was an increase in confidence as language users because they realized that they were able to communicate appropriately. In turn, this realization boosted their confidence as language learners. At the end of the experience, each participant was asked to write a semi-structured reflection on their VE experience. From content analysis, four main themes arose.

Theme 1: Cultural Gains

All students explicitly stated that the experience allowed them to learn about other cultures. For example, one student wrote: "I learned that there are a variety of differences between our cultures, such as local crisis, life in college and local foods. These are aspects that define the cultural context of the other person" (Student 12). Likewise, some students were surprised to learn that their cultural differences were not as pronounced as they had expected. For instance, Student 15 mentioned that she did not notice "many cultural differences; we share tastes and ways of thinking, and it is easy to understand each other."

In our analysis, we noticed that students not only referred to superficial aspects of the culture such as food and celebrations but also deeper aspects such as values, beliefs, and family relationships. This awareness of deep cultural aspects may be due not only to the activities that required students to explore less apparent aspects of culture but also to the connection that they developed with their partners, allowing them to ask questions about more sensitive or controversial topics that they might not ask in different circumstances.

For instance, there were discussions that extended from the use of certain words that were deemed as inappropriate by the U.S. L1 English users. In some cases, the equivalent of these words in Spanish are used by Colombians as terms of endearment. With such conflicting views, Colombian students used these conversations as an opportunity to get a glimpse of the current complex racial issues of the United States and the influence these issues have on the language used by their counterparts in the United States. At the same time, there were many enlightening experiences on the side of the students in the United States who were not familiar with common (and usually taken for granted) aspects of Colombian life, such as the concept of *estratos*, which formally and legally divides all aspects of society according to household financial capacity. The *estratos* discussion brought up the deeply rooted influence of money on all aspects of Colombian society. One of the discussion points was that it is inappropriate to ask about socioeconomic background in the United States (particularly in job-related or social settings), while in Colombia it is common. On the other hand, in Colombia it is extremely unusual to ask about or include race in a government form or CV—and most people would not know how to answer what race they belonged to—while in the United States it is standard on forms (but not in other situations). Both topics, class and race, are usually taboo conversations in both contexts, but the dynamics of the VEs provided a safe and friendly environment to learn about and discuss them.

Theme 2: Language Improvement

Students also highlighted the development of their language skills. They reported that they were able to practice what they had learned in class in different ways. Students reported that they improved their writing (for those who chose to write letters) (n=15; 42 percent), pronunciation (n=4; 11 percent), and listening skills (n=15; 42 percent). Additionally, about 55 percent (n=20) of the students highlighted the importance of providing and receiving explicit feedback. One student summarized this when she reflected, "The experience was very good; it helped me to improve a lot in terms of my writing thanks to the feedback that my e-pal did" (Student 16). This student also reported that she and her partner mutually learned from the peer feedback phase of the exchange since each participant was expected to correct any errors made in the target language. Similarly, Student 10 indicated that "speaking in his [partner's] language was one of the main challenges, and I received a lot of help from him so that I could correct my mistakes." The same benefit was seen in previous studies (García, Rey, & Rosado, 2009, 2010; Mizuno et al., 2006; Rey, & Rosado, 2001; O'Rourke, 2005).

Theme 3: Pragmatics

As the emphasis of the course was on intercultural communication, about half of the students (n=18) observed that they used culturally appropriate communication strategies. As Student 5 stated, "Through the experience I was able to put into practice what I learned in class, how to interact, how to behave and strategies for a good communication with the other culture." Many students (n=14; 39 percent) also mentioned that they learned to be respectful and keep an open mind toward their peers; these aspects are essential parts of intercultural learning. An example of this can be seen in Student 13's reflection: "This experience taught me to be open minded and respectful so we can interact with people from other cultures." This finding agrees with the conclusions of Belz (2003), who suggests that VEs promote the development of intercultural competences among geographically dispersed students.

Theme 4: Language Awareness

An emerging category of analysis was that of "language awareness"; some students ($n=11$; 31 percent) valued the activity because it allowed them (for the first time, in many cases) to acknowledge their ability to use the language in a context beyond the EFL classroom. Thus, they felt a sense of achievement and became more confident when interacting in English. An example of this can be seen from Student 25, who said that it was hard to write in his own language, Spanish, and he "thought that in English it would be more complicated, but it was not so." In the same vein, another student said: "[The VE] made me lose my fear of speaking a little and become more sure of the things I say, since on many occasions they [the partners] expressed that I have a very good command of the language [English], so that was satisfactory for me" (Student 16). VEs provided students with real communication opportunities, and the resulting interaction, contact, and validation helped learners to become more aware of their capability to communicate in English.

Student Challenges

Alongside the many positive outcomes of the VE experience, students also encountered some difficulties. One of the most prevalent was scheduling video chat meetings. Because students had different schedules and commitments, ten students reported having issues reaching a consensus on the times and dates of the virtual meetings. As Student 18 recalled: "A challenge I remember is to agree on the time for the video call. Sometimes they [VE partner] could not meet, it was either too late for them or too early for me, or there were certain inconveniences on the platform (we tried to communicate twice), but the important thing is that we found a space that allowed us to meet through video." This challenge was more of an issue than it might normally be due to the fact that many U.S. college students have jobs, which is not the case for the majority of Colombian students. This issue caused some anxiety since the students had deadlines to complete the assignments.

Of the 36 student participants, eight mentioned that they had to be "patient" with their partners because of their "low level" of Spanish. Thus, some felt frustrated and eventually ended up using English as the main means of communication in the virtual exchanges. Student 32 expressed that "it was a bit frustrating that they [U.S. partners] did not speak our language [Spanish] so well, and that the jargon they used was more formal [. . .] and it is strange, since we do not usually speak as formally as they are taught." Despite this, students were generally able to handle their frustration. The level of formality in speech and other subtle pragmatic aspects were non-linguistic or cultural skills; in real communication settings, speakers are likely to interact with speakers at different language proficiency levels.

These difficulties are not unique to this study (O'Dowd, 2013; Starke-Meyerring & Wilson, 2008). For future iterations of VE, more consideration would be needed in such areas as matching students according to availability and warning students about possible sources of conflict, including differences in language level and issues with platforms.

Implications for Policy, Practice, and Future Research

This study provides evidence that VEs are a highly attractive endeavor for language learners in terms of equity of access, as all students in the language course were involved, not only those with the resources and opportunity to travel abroad. Furthermore, in terms of intercultural competences, the VEs have great potential to generate positive changes that allow students to interact and compare their culture with that of a language learner from another country. These competencies can be the core of future courses with a similar scope and include: *knowing the other*, which refers to what they learned from the other culture; *knowing themselves*, which relates to learning about themselves in relation to the other; and *interacting with their partner*, which can be associated with the interplay between the two students speaking different languages. In fact, students in this study felt that they learned not only about superficial topics but also deeper cultural issues, which was one of the goals of the course. The VE promoted a closer relationship between students by allowing them to explore issues (i.e., family relationships, political views, ethics, values) that are not commonly discussed by people just getting to know each other but that more closely replicate those in a face-to-face study abroad experience. We found that learning about some types of hidden or taboo cultural aspects that were otherwise usually revealed only in study abroad experiences or visits may be possible through virtual exchanges. This finding opens the door to encourage these types of detailed and culturally relevant conversations as part of the VEs in a respectful and safe way.

In addition to these intercultural benefits, students reported developing their communicative competence, which may be attributed to the fact that VEs provided them with opportunities to communicate for authentic purposes. Students realized that they could actually communicate in English with real speakers of the target language, which gave them a sense of achievement and boosted their confidence to use English. Not only could they use the language, but they were also able to make their own choices to interact interculturally, which their partners assessed as being culturally appropriate or not. This led to a more educated selection of strategies that took into account cultural differences and the language proficiency of their partners. But learning to deal with these types of challenges and frustrations is inherent to building intercultural competence and having authentic communication across cultures. Likewise, students on both sides experienced practical challenges related to scheduling and time management conflicts, as well as handling frustration related to miscommunication between languages.

Although these types of experiences have been implemented for at least two decades, mainly in language teaching (Arnold & Fonseca-Mora, 2015), VE has recently been revitalized not only by the ubiquitous use of and widespread access to the internet but more recently by the enforced remote and virtual learning situations derived from the COVID-19 lockdowns and travel restrictions. In fact, recent surveys and reports (Gutterer, 2020; Quacquarelli Symonds, 2020a, 2020b) on the impact of COVID-19 on study plans (local and abroad) reveal that even with the ease on travel restrictions and safety measures, students in general are less likely to engage in study abroad plans. In the wake of the pandemic fears and as the world establishes new protocols and travel restrictions around the world, VEs can be one part of virtual study abroad initiatives, as reported by Durden (2020), especially in those programs with mobility requirements. Moreover, new communication technologies derived from the internet that allow learners to communicate in real time with peers in different parts of the world are spreading to other disciplines, such as engineering, business administration, and medicine (Abdel-Kader, 2020; O'Dowd, 2018).

VEs have important implications not only for language students but also for language instructors and curricula (see Bush, Allen, Farner, & Pimenova, this volume). Instructors can also develop new competencies during the VE experience as they negotiate with the teaching partner from a different culture (as was our case). Deciding on a partner university and selecting the partner instructor is an important decision, since a strong relationship is required to set up and plan a practical and satisfactory experience. We implemented the virtual exchanges with a U.S. institution that our university already had worked with in smaller-scale projects. From our experience, VEs seem to be most successful with institutions that have worked well together previously or with professors who already have some type of professional or personal relationship. However, some universities may not have established alliances, and faculty may need to connect with interested colleagues via open virtual exchange platforms, such as Columbus Hub Academy.

We have continued implementing our VE with our partner institution and have found that in each iteration, logistics and curricular alignment have become easier to manage in spite of situations requiring adjustments. At the beginning, we were more ambitious with the number of weeks over which the VE took place. With experience, we found that less time and more focused activities were more effective for student engagement and learning. Also, when faced with a change in course assignment or a difference in course calendars, professors worked together to adjust the themes, learning outcomes, and tasks. In terms of curriculum, we learned that it is essential to match learning outcomes, themes or topics, and activities that will be carried out while educating students on the importance of the experience. One way to provide this motivation is by aligning course assessment with the activities of the experience, as we did. In light of this, we recommend flexibility on both sides of the experience when aligning curriculum, academic calendars, deadlines, and tasks.

We also recommend that educators incorporate appropriate assessments as part of the integration of VEs into a curriculum. Well planned evaluations allow educators to make more robust claims about the impact of VEs on student learning, which should be measured by all means available, including objective interculturality inventories, proficiency tests, and qualitative measures such as the ones used in this study. Future research should explore the effect of VEs on formal aspects of academic learning, including curricular adjustments and syllabi, assessment practices, instruments to measure the goals of the VE, and teacher education. VEs may be innovative and (most times) "fun," but the rationale for their use extends much further. In fact, VEs are the product of many contemporary views on language, learners, and learning platform technology.

APPENDIX 4A: Statements on International/Intercultural Competencies in Pre-/Post-Survey

Statement
1. I can identify the culture I belong to and the meaning of belonging to it.
2. I can identify the beliefs and attitudes of other cultures.
3. I can appreciate positive aspects of my own cultural heritage and recognize how these can help me to understand cultural differences.
4. I consider it necessary to know about other cultures and be sensitive to them.
5. I can identify the attitudes, beliefs and values that show my respect and appreciation toward other cultures.
6. I can identify the attitudes, beliefs and values that prevent me from respecting or appreciating other cultures.
7. I will try to correct the attitudes and beliefs that prevent me from respecting and appreciating the differences with other ethnic groups and cultures.
8. I know my cultural heritage, for example, the ethnic group, the language and the history of my ancestors.
9. I can identify, at least, 5 characteristics of my own culture and explain how these affect my relationship with people from my own culture and from others
10. I can identify common aspects with other cultures that help me to respect and value them.
11. I can describe a situation in which I have offended someone for these reasons: racism, prejudices, discrimination, and stereotypes.

12. When I interact with people from other cultures, I try to learn as much as I can from them to avoid behaviors that can lead to discrimination

13. When I interact with people from other cultures, I can recognize behaviors that lead to discrimination.

14. I can relate to people from different cultural backgrounds and maintain a dialogue about culture differences and preferences.

15. I maintain good relationships with individuals who belong to a cultural group different from my own, and I participate in open dialogue that gives me feedback on my behavior.

16. I recognize that I have stereotypes (pre-established ideas) about people who belong to a cultural group different from my own.

17. I can give examples of how my stereotypes (pre-established ideas) can affect my relationships with other people.

18. I can give an example of positive or negative emotional reactions toward other cultural groups and how these have influenced my behavior.

REFERENCES

Adbel-Kadel, M. (2020, April 14). Harnessing technology for global education. *Inside Higher Ed.* Retrieved from https://www.insidehighered.com/views/2020/04/14/colleges -should-develop-more-virtual-exchange-programs-maintain-and-increase-global

Arnold, J., & Fonseca-Mora, M. C. (2015). Language and cultural encounters: Opportunities for interaction with native speakers. In D. Nunan & J. C. Richards (Eds.), *Language learning beyond the classroom* (pp. 225–234). New York: Routledge.

Baker, L., & Brown, A.L. (1984). Metacognitive skills and reading. In P.D. Pearson, R. Barr, M.L. Kamil, & P. Mosenthal (Eds.), *Handbook of reading research* (pp. 353–394). New York: Longman.

Barksdale, M. A., Watson, C., & Park, E. S. (2007). Pen pal letter exchanges: Taking first steps toward developing cultural understandings. *The Reading Teacher, 61*(1), 58–68.

Beelen, J., & Jones, E. (2015). Looking back at the 15 years of Internationalization at Home. *EAIE Forum,* 6–8.

Belz, J. (2003). Linguistic perspectives on the development of intercultural competence in telecollaboration. *Language Learning & Technology, 7*(2), 68–99.

Belz, J. (2007). The development of intercultural communicative competence in telecollaborative partnerships. In R. O'Dowd (Ed.) *Online intercultural exchange: An introduction for foreign language teachers* (pp. 127–166). Clevendon, England: Multilingual Matters.

Byram, M. (1997). *Teaching and assessing intercultural communicative competence.* Clevendon, England: Multilingual Matters.

Cano, J., & Ricardo, C. (2014). *Instrumento para el análisis de la competencia intercultural en estudiantes de educación superior.* Unpublished doctoral diss., Universidad del Norte, Barranquilla, Colombia.

Cohen, L., Manion, L., & Morrison, K. (2011). *Research methods in education* (7th ed.). Oxford, England: Routledge.

Creswell, J. W. (2003). *Research design: Qualitative, quantitative, and mixed method approaches* (2nd ed.). Thousand Oaks, CA: Sage.

Creswell, J. W. (2014). *A concise introduction to mixed methods research.* Thousand Oaks, CA: Sage.

Denzin, N. K., & Lincoln, Y. (Eds.). (2018). *The Sage handbook of qualitative research.* Thousand Oaks, CA: Sage.

Durden, W.G. (2020, June 4). Here's a new way to do study abroad during the COVID-19 pandemic and beyond. *The Conversation.* Retrieved from https://theconversation .com/heres-a-new-way-to-do-study-abroad-during-the-covid-19-pandemic-and -beyond-138931

Elo, S., Kaarianinen, M., Kanste, O., Polkki, R., Utriainen, K., & Kyngas, H. (2014). Qualitative Content Analysis: A focus on trustworthiness. *Journal of Mixed Methods Research, 1*(2), 112–133.

Fuchs, C., Hauck, M., & Müller-Hartmann, A. (2012). Promoting learner autonomy through multiliteracy skills development in cross-institutional exchanges. *Language Learning & Technology, 16*(3), 82–102. Retrieved from http://llt.msu.edu/issues/october 2012/fuchsetal.pdf

García, M., Rey, L., & Rosado, N. (2010). El intercambio virtual y el desarrollo de las competencias lingüísticas e intercultural (Tomo 3, Parte 2, Cap. 1). In A. De Castro (Ed.). *Innovar para educar: Prácticas universitarias exitosas* (pp. 40–51). Barranquilla, Colombia: Ediciones Uninorte.

García, M., Rey, L., & Rosado, N. (2009). Intercambio virtual: Impacto en el desarrollo de las competencias lingüísticas e interculturales. *Zona Próxima, 11*, 122–133.

Gläsman, S. (2004). *Communication online.* Bedfordbury, England: CILT.

Gutterer, J. (2020). The impact of COVID-19 on international students perceptions–Part 2: The perception gap between studying at home and abroad. *Study Portals.* Retrieved from https://studyportals.com/?p=17956

Helm, F. (2015). The practices and challenges of telecollaboration in higher education in Europe. *Language Learning & Technology, 19*(2), 197–217.

Helm, F. (2019). Languages and international virtual exchange: Introduction to the special issue. *European Journal of Language Policy, 11*(2), 139–142.

Kötter, M. (2003) Negotiation of meaning and codeswitching in online tandems. *Language Learning & Technology, 7*(2): 145–172.

Lee, L. (2006). A study of native and nonnative speakers' feedback and responses in Spanish-American networked collaborative interaction. In J. A. Belz & S. L.Thorne (Eds.) *Internet-mediated intercultural foreign language education* (pp. 147–176). Boston: Thomson Heinle.

Lemkuhl, M. (2002). Pen-pal letters: The cross-curricular experience. *The Reading Teacher, 55*(8), 720–722.

López-Rocha, S. (2016). Intercultural communicative competence: creating awareness and promoting skills in the language classroom. In C. Goria, O. Speicher, & S. Stollhans (Eds), *Innovative language teaching and learning at university: Enhancing participation and collaboration* (pp. 105–111). Dublin, Ireland: Research-publishing.net. http://dx.doi.org/10.14705/rpnet.2016.000399

Mizuno, J, Jánica, D., Rey, L., & Rosado, N. (2006). A multimedia material for effective transcultural learning. *Zona Próxima, 7*, 12–39.

Möllering, M., & Levy, M. (2012). Intercultural competence in computer-mediated communication: An analysis of research methods. In M. Dooly & R. O'Dowd (Eds.) *Researching online foreign language interaction and exchange* (pp.135–162). Bern, Switzerland: Peter Lang.

O'Dowd, R. (2013). Telecollaboration and CALL. In M. Thomas, H. Reindeers, & M. Warschauer (Eds.). *Contemporary computer-assisted language learning* (pp. 123–141). London: Bloomsbury Academic.

O'Dowd, R., & Lewis, T. (Eds.) (2016) *Online intercultural exchange: Policy, pedagogy, practice.* New York: Routledge.

O'Dowd, R. (2017). Virtual exchange and internationalising the classroom. *Training Language and Culture, 1*(4), 8–24.

O'Dowd, R. (2018). From telecollaboration to virtual exchange: State-of-the-art and the role of UNICollaboration in moving forward. *Journal of Virtual Exchange, 1*, 1–23.

O'Rourke, B. (2005). Form-focused Interaction in online tandem learning. *CALICO Journal, 22*(3), 433–466.

Pellettieri, J. (2000). Negotiation in cyberspace: The role of chatting in the development of grammatical competence. In M. Warschauer & R. Kern (Eds.). *Network-based language teaching: Concepts and practice* (pp. 59–87). Cambridge, England: Cambridge University Press.

Quacquarelli Symonds. (2020a). The impact of the coronavirus on prospective international students. *QS.* Retrieved from https://www.qs.com/portfolio-items/how-covid -19-is-impacting-prospective-international-students-across-the-globe

Quacquarelli Symonds. (2020b). How COVID-19 is impacting prospective international students across the globe. *QS*. Retrieved from https://www.qs.com/portfolio-items/the-impact-of-the-coronavirus-on-prospective-international-students/

Rey, L., & Rosado, N. (2001). Empowering the EFL/ESL class through e-mail activities. *Zona Próxima* (2), 10–23.

Starke-Meyerring, D., & Wilson, M. (Eds). (2008). *Designing globally networked learning environments: Visionary partnerships, policies, and pedagogies*. Rotterdam, Netherlands: Sense Publishers.

Schenker, T. (2017). Synchronous telecollaboration for novice language learners: Effects on speaking skills and language learning interests. *Alsic, 20*(2). https://doi.org/10.4000/alsic.3068

Tian, J., & Wang, Y. (2010). Taking language learning outside the classroom: Learners' perspectives of eTandem learning via Skype. *Innovation in Language Learning and Teaching, 4*(3), 181–197.

Wells, G. (1996, February). Making meaning with text: A generic approach to the mediated role of writing in activity. Paper presented at the meeting of the Assembly on Research, Vygotsky Centennial: Vygotskian Perspectives on Literacy Research, Chicago.

Yamada, M. (2009). The role of social presence in learner-centered communicative language learning using synchronous computer-mediated communication: Experimental study. *Computers & Education, 52*(4), 820–833.

5

Enhancing Internationalization at Home through Undergraduates Volunteering for an ITA Program

Lixia Cheng

Internationalization in higher education has been defined as "the process of integrating an international, intercultural or global dimension into the purpose, functions or delivery of post-secondary education" (Knight, 2003, p. 2). Internationalization differs considerably across institutions in terms of strategic planning and actual implementations. This chapter joins academic discussions about internationalization by featuring Purdue University, a public university with world renowned STEM programs and consistently large numbers of international students. As a Tier 1 research institution in the United States, Purdue University takes pride in its "rich cultural diversity" and increasing global impact through research collaborations and academic mobility of students and faculty (Purdue University, n.d.b; Neubert, 2015). In fact, Purdue has boasted the second to fourth largest enrollments of international students among all U.S. public universities in the most recent decade (Purdue University, n.d.a). Throughout its long-term internationalization process, Purdue has strived to meet major programming needs, such as providing appropriate language and cultural support to international students since the first half of the 20th century and promoting cultural integration and academic collaboration between domestic and international students in the most recent decade (Haan, 2009; Neubert, 2015).

This chapter presents a historical account of internationalization efforts at Purdue, particularly in respect to offering ESL support to international students, followed by a focus on a curricular component implemented by an on-campus ESL support program, the Oral English Proficiency Program (OEPP), to connect international teaching assistant (ITA) candidates and domestic undergraduate students. The OEPP tests and certifies the oral English proficiency of prospective ITAs and offers a "Classroom Communication in ESL" course to graduate students who failed the in-house Oral English Proficiency Test (OEPT). The objectives of this course are to enhance ITA candidates' instructional and interpersonal communicative abilities, which are essential skills for successful interaction with domestic students in undergraduate classes, lab or recitation sessions, and office hours.

Issues and Challenges That Motivated the Research

Since around 2011, Purdue has consistently ranked among the top five U.S. public universities with the largest international student population; since the late 1980s, it has also established and sustained several ESL support programs on and around campus. In addition to tracing these efforts by Purdue to internationalize its main campus over time, I investigate whether and how internationalization at home (IaH), a cost-effective subset of internationalization, has evolved at the university. IaH aims to produce globally minded and interculturally adept university students—domestic and international—through "purposeful integration of international and intercultural dimensions into the formal and informal curriculum for all students within domestic learning environments" (Beelen & Jones, 2015, p. 69). Specific questions related to IaH at Purdue may include how the university has internationalized teaching and learning to facilitate the sociocultural integration of international students into the university and to equip domestic students with international knowledge, skills, and attitudes.

In relation to Purdue's IaH efforts, some ESL programs on campus have embedded a contact component into their curricula to connect international students with native English-speaking students or local residents. Two notable examples are: (1) the two versions of a Language Partner Program (LPP) implemented by the PLaCE program (see Bush, Allen, Farner, & Pimenova, this volume) for promoting linguistic and cultural interactions between undergraduate international students and domestic students; and (2) instructional activities organized in 2012–2013 by the then-coordinator of University Residences' English for Speakers of Other Languages (ESOL) program. An activity included in the PLaCE LPP grouped one Chinese language student with two first-year PLaCE Chinese students and engaged them in language and culture sharing through lexicogrammar exercises and conversations structured around a prompt. Likewise, the ESOL students—mostly spouses of graduate students living in Purdue Village apartments—presented posters as part of their ESOL class to introduce their home culture to a group of Purdue University retirees and other local senior citizens (B. Lageveen, personal communication, November 2013).

Contact components, such as these instructional activities incorporated into the PLaCE LPP and the ESOL courses, have mostly been studied from the perspective of the interaction hypothesis, with a focus on how the interaction might benefit second language acquisition (e.g., Long, 1996; Plonsky & Gass, 2011; Ziegler, 2016). Comparatively, much less attention has been paid to the effect on the other party, such as the Chinese language students participating in the PLaCE LPP or the local senior citizens invited to the cross-cultural poster presentations in the ESOL class. It seems that the only empirical research about the effect on the other party in these carefully designed encounter situations was conducted by Staples, Kang, and Wittner (2014), who, through a quasi-experimental, pre-/post-test design, found that institutionally supported, structured contact between prospective ITAs and U.S. undergraduate volunteers had positive impacts on volunteers' outcome ratings of audio-recorded teaching presentations by ITA candidates regarding accent, comprehensibility, and teaching ability.

The lack of research on how interaction with ITA candidates may impact domestic undergraduate students' intercultural development became my initial motivation for studying the volunteer program in the OEPP, a long-standing ITA support program at Purdue. Therefore, this chapter will first provide an overview of the OEPP volunteer program, starting with a narrative about the establishment of the OEPP as a crisis management resolution to undergraduates' complaints about ITAs' incomprehensible, accented speech. Then, I will turn the spotlight on a mature, impactful volunteer program that has become an integral part of the ITA training course offered by the OEPP, with close attention paid to how both parties in the linguistic and cultural interactions perceive the volunteer program.

Historical Developments

In general, the gradual internationalization of Purdue's main campus reflected a larger national trend. In the years after World War I when the United States began to be seen as a new leading destination for top international students due to the country's strong economy and intellectual resources, Purdue witnessed an increase from 18 to 65 international students between 1918 and 1924 and a greater diversity in the students' ethno-geographical backgrounds, which ranged from Latin America to Asia (Purdue University, 1918; Purdue University, 1924).

However, concerns about international students' English language competence, or lack thereof, were not addressed until the early 1920s amidst Purdue faculty's continuous complaints about some domestic students' difficulties with academic English. In response, international students were offered a remedial English course designed for domestic students that functioned as the prerequisite for the equivalent of today's first-year composition course (Haan, 2009). This contingency plan lasted only a few years until English B, the first non-credit English course including writing and speaking skills, was developed in 1926 by an assistant professor of English to be taught exclusively to international graduate and undergraduate students to help them achieve "satisfactory performance of their general university work" (Purdue University, 1926). International students who excelled in English B were granted credit for first-year composition (i.e., English 1). Even though its international enrollments in the 1920s were not as impressive as those of peer institutions, Purdue seemed to have been the pioneer in the early provision of a custom-made English support course for international students (Haan, 2009).

After a steady fivefold increase in international enrollments across the nation from post–World War II until the 1960s, the budget reductions for higher education in the early 1970s gave rise to arguments against recruiting international students (Sutton, 1971). International students were argued to lower the standards of U.S. college education and eventually cause a "brain drain" once these U.S.-educated students graduate and return home. International education was perceived as "a symbol of the rising competitive challenge of former foes and so-called Third World nations" (O'Mara, 2012, p. 609). Consequently, individual universities were left to make and defend their own decisions about international recruitment and solve the "problem" of English deficiency that some international students faced.

At Purdue, the non-credit English B course remained the only language support for international undergraduate and graduate students from 1926 until 1955. Later improvement in English language support for international students included (1) the addition in 1955 of a two-hour lab session to English B's original three-hour class design; (2) the separation of English B in 1976 into a three-credit first-year composition course for international undergraduate students and a six-hour non-credit course for graduate students, and (3) the addition in 1979 of a remedial language course functioning as the prerequisite for first-year composition (Haan, 2009).

The year 1979 also marked the first official recognition of international graduate students as "a significant and valuable segment of the academic community at Purdue University" in the 160-page *Report on International Education and Research at Purdue University* presented to the University Senate (p. 56). However, this report also raised the issue of international graduate teaching assistants' English proficiency. Due to petitions and media coverage showing domestic students' and parents' resentment about incomprehensible lectures and unfair grades, the nationwide "ITA problem" became the driving force for state mandates across the United States on the certification of ITA candidates' English proficiency, which created the need for institutions to provide support for ITAs.

As a public university with the mission of serving Indiana residents, Purdue's response to its own ITA situation was to create an ITA preparation course, English 001t in 1981 and a four-week intensive pilot course in 1985. The OEPP, a university-wide ITA-preparation program, was founded in 1987 and started to offer intermediate and advanced English classes, which were consolidated in 2000 into one course that students could repeat if their proficiency was still below par at the end of the semester.

The ITA Preparation Course and Undergraduate Volunteer Program

The most recent course-offering pattern has been that 10–14 sections of the five-credit pass/fail OEPP class are offered in a regular fall or spring semester and one or two sections are offered in summer. An instructor and a tutor are teamed up to teach each section of eight ITA candidates. Every ITA student participates in two two-hour class sessions with the instructor and all classmates every week, in addition to a 30-minute individual conference with the instructor and a 50-minute one-on-one tutorial with the tutor.

The curriculum for the OEPP class (English 620, "Classroom Communication in ESL for Teaching Assistants") has remained relatively stable since the early 2000s. Besides practicing interpersonal communication (e.g., small talk, turn-taking, leave-taking), every ITA student placed into English 620 is expected to give four 20-minute presentations in front of their instructor, classmates, and undergraduate volunteers. These presentations are formal, rehearsed, and distributed throughout the semester. The target language tasks are to introduce the student's field of study in the first presentation, explain a term in their field in the second and third presentations, and introduce the syllabus for an undergraduate class in the final presentation.

Since 2014, an OEPP senior lecturer has been designated the volunteer coordinator to recruit undergraduate volunteers for these presentations, which are organized into 50-minute sessions. In each session, volunteers watch two presentations, interact with presenters during a question-and-answer portion, and then evaluate and comment on each presentation using the form provided by the OEPP (see Appendix 5A). Another curricular component needing volunteers is one 50-minute mid-semester "Cookies and Conversation" roundtable during which undergraduate volunteers engage in relaxed conversations with English 620 students. Common topics discussed in this roundtable include experiences with and expectations for ITAs, as well as the campus culture as it relates to being an international graduate student or an undergraduate at Purdue.

The OEPP set the goal for the volunteer coordinator to recruit at least five undergraduate volunteers for each presentation session. More recent incentivization efforts include reaching out to larger undergraduate courses such as Communication 114, whose teaching faculty may be willing to offer extra credit or make OEPP volunteering an option for a service project. A second incentive has been to award an OEPP-issued Intercultural Communication Partner certificate to volunteers who have contributed a certain number of hours during an academic year to support ITA candidates in English 620. Undergraduate students can earn volunteer hours through observing English 620 presentation sessions and/or participating in the mid-semester "Cookies and Conversation" roundtable (B. Lageveen, personal communication, August 2019).

Research Questions

Building on the historical review of Purdue's internationalization and provision of ESL support up to when the OEPP was founded in the late 1980s, I report on an exploratory study investigating how campus internationalization is currently realized and enhanced through an IaH component in the English 620 curriculum at Purdue. The IaH is implemented by domestic undergraduate students' participation in the OEPP volunteer program. Based on the themes emerging from my qualitative, exploratory research process, these questions were developed:

1. How is internationalization actualized when domestic undergraduate students volunteer in the OEPP curricular

activities? What is the scope of domestic undergraduate students' involvement in these volunteer activities in support of ITA candidates?

2. How do interactants on both sides—domestic undergraduate volunteers and ITA candidates—perceive the value of these volunteer activities?

Answers to these research questions provide valuable insight to ESL program directors and university administrators in similar contexts about a viable and practical approach to implementing and enhancing IaH.

Research Methods

The primary methods adopted in this study are document research and personal communication with relevant staff members at Purdue. The list of materials surveyed include (1) archival documents about the university's history of internationalization and provision of ESL support, (2) the recruitment flyers and advocacy video created and used by the OEPP volunteer coordinator, (3) the materials given to undergraduate volunteers participating in the OEPP class, and (4) other records and files related to the OEPP volunteer program.

Most of the materials related to the OEPP volunteer program were from 2014 to 2019, except for the aggregated summary reports on the OEPP internal surveys administered to all English 620 students in the fall semesters of 2008, 2013, and 2015. The two YouTube videos used to promote the volunteer program are accessible via links on the OEPP website (https://www.purdue.edu/oepp/volunteer/index.html). The stakeholders include Purdue faculty and students seeking ideas for a service project; instructors encouraging undergraduate students to interact with ITAs; and undergraduate students interested in learning about ITAs, practicing intercultural communication, and building their résumé through these volunteer activities.

For volunteer registration, the OEPP uses a multi-functional web application, developed by a third-party software company, to allow undergraduate volunteers to easily view available dates and time for volunteering, sign up for one or more slots, and receive automatic confirmation and reminders. This web application facilitates recordkeeping so that the OEPP staff can track the volunteer hours per individual for the purposes of issuing certificates and thank-you notes.

Findings and Discussion

Format and Scope of OEPP Volunteer Program

My analysis of available data indicates that IaH can be achieved through the OEPP volunteer program, which consists of two curricular components. In the first type of volunteer activity, undergraduate volunteers observe a 50-minute presentation session, ask questions during the question-and-answer portion, and provide written feedback to the two ITA candidates who present during the session. In the second type of volunteer activity, undergraduate volunteers act as conversation partners in a 50-minute mid-semester "Cookies and Conversation" roundtable.

To solicit useful feedback from undergraduate volunteers for ITA candidates on their instructional presentation, the OEPP has developed an information sheet and an evaluation form for undergraduate volunteers (see Appendix 5A). The information sheet provides general guidelines and specific language expressions to guide the volunteers' commentary that will be input on the evaluation form along with analytic ratings. It is worth noting that the information sheet aligns with the course curriculum, especially concerning the important categories involved in giving a teaching presentation, such as the explanation of presentation objectives and the use of examples. Likewise, the five levels on the evaluation form align with the five-point OEPT holistic rating scale, which has become a core part of the standardized language testing and classroom assessments implemented in the OEPP. The five-point OEPT rating scale of 35-40-45-50-55 is familiar to English 620 students because they review their OEPT test performance with their instructor and tutor at the beginning of the semester. English 620 instructors are also very familiar with this scale because instructors are trained OEPT test raters.

To better prepare ITA candidates for giving instructional presentations, the OEPP has compiled a list of common constructive feedback provided by undergraduate volunteers to ITA student presenters in the English 620 course (see Appendix 5B). This collection of volunteers' feedback also conveys certain parts of the U.S. academic culture, including domestic undergraduates' expectations and practices, such as "show that you want to teach and are motivated to do so" and "we would never tell you that you are pronouncing a word incorrectly unless we have your permission to do so."

In terms of the scope of the OEPP volunteer program, a total of 1,536 undergraduate students signed up in the 2017–2018 academic year for either observing one or more 50-minute presentation sessions or participating in the 50-minute mid-semester "Cookies and Conversation" roundtable discussions with ITA candidates in the English 620 course. They spent a total of 2,869 volunteer hours in the English 620 classrooms (Kauper, 2019). This suggests that on average, each of these 1,536 undergraduate volunteers contributed to two 50-minute volunteer sessions during the 2017–2018 academic year. In the 2020–2021 COVID-19 pandemic year, the volunteer tracking system registered a total of 1,177 volunteer hours completed by 590 students.

Interactants' Perceptions about the Value of the OEPP Volunteer Program

In the first and major type of volunteer activity, ITA candidates simulate teaching an undergraduate class where undergraduate students may request clarification or ask a follow-up question after the ITA's presentation/lecture. This interaction between the ITA candidate and undergraduate audience members is a great opportunity for the ITA candidate to practice listening and speaking skills, as well as the ability to teach in English. The encounter also provides for some intercultural experience for both the ITA candidate and the undergraduate volunteer.

In the YouTube video advocating for the OEPP volunteer program, one domestic undergraduate mechanical engineering student who had volunteered 64 hours in the 2017–2018 academic year shared her testimony: "I really enjoy volunteering because it's fun to meet a lot of the international students, and also I really like learning the things that they have to teach me." She went on to explain why she considered it important for undergraduate students like herself to volunteer in the OEPP English 620 class: "I think it's very likely that you'll see one of these graduate students as your TA in the future, so by giving them feedback you could actually be helping yourself when they come back to be your TA" (OEPP, 2019).

This undergraduate volunteer emphasized the academic benefit she received during the volunteering process (e.g., she learned some interesting things about a subject matter not necessarily in her field of study) and the potential academic benefit of getting improved instruction from an ITA in the future due to the constructive feedback these pre-service ITAs received from undergraduate volunteers. Overall, this undergraduate volunteer found it enjoyable to meet a lot of the international graduate students at Purdue and volunteer as an audience member to help ITA candidates improve their instructional presentations.

The advocacy video also shows how the other party—namely, ITA candidates in the English 620 course—might perceive these linguistic and intercultural interactions with undergraduate volunteers. A South Korean civil engineering graduate student said, "Through that [English 620] course, I could interact more with undergraduate students. Actually, before that, I was nervous when I'm [was] interacting with undergraduate student[s]. But after taking that course, I could be more comfortable and confident when I'm talking with undergraduate students. I think it is helpful for being a TA in Purdue University" (OEPP, 2019).

This graduate student emphasized the positive influence of interacting with undergraduate volunteers in terms of helping her overcome nervousness that she used to have whenever speaking with domestic undergraduate students. The positive attitudes that ITA candidates hold toward the volunteer program were echoed in English 620 students' anonymous responses to a program-wide comprehensive course survey that the OEPP conducts every few years. Aggregated reports on the survey distribution in the fall semesters of 2008, 2013, and 2015 show that an average of 96 percent of all survey respondents across the three years strongly agreed or agreed with the statement: "Having undergrads in the audience during [English] 620 presentations was a valuable experience" (OEPP, 2016).

Compared to observing two ITA candidates' instructional presentations in a 50-minute English 620 class session, the second type of OEPP volunteer activity (i.e., participating in one 50-minute mid-semester "Cookies and Conversation" roundtable) is less formal, less academic, and less structured. The aggregated reports on the internal, comprehensive English 620 course surveys included three questions about the curricular component with the undergraduate roundtable. In contrast, there was only one question about having undergraduate volunteers in the English 620 presentation sessions because presentation as a category of learning activities in the course encompasses a few other areas to survey English 620 students about (e.g., using presentation skills learned in English 620 outside this class, feeling more confident in handling question-and-answer situations).

Table 5.1 lists the four questions related to the OEPP volunteer program on the comprehensive course surveys administered in the fall of 2008, 2013, and 2015. This internal comprehensive course survey has

TABLE 5.1: OEPP Volunteer Program-Related Questions on English 620 Comprehensive Course Survey Administered Falls 2008, 2013, and 2015

Item # on Internal Course Survey	Category	Statement*	2008	2013	2015
			Strongly Agree + Agree (percentage)		
26	Presentation	Having undergrads in the audience during 620 presentations was a valuable experience.	94%	98%	96%
38	UG Roundtable	The undergraduate roundtable helped me understand undergraduate culture at Purdue.	*	76%	88%
39	UG Roundtable	I liked the undergraduate roundtable.	54%	81%	86%
40	UG Roundtable	The undergraduate roundtable was a valuable use of class time.	56%	85%	87%

*Some statements were not part of the 2008 survey.
Source: OEPP (2016).

been administered only occasionally because the English 620 curriculum has remained stable since the early 2000s and OEPP administrators want to avoid survey fatigue on the part of English 620 students—considering that there is an end-of-the-semester teaching effectiveness survey distributed by the Center for Instructional Excellence to students in any credit-bearing course at Purdue. As indicated, "The undergraduate roundtable helped me understand undergraduate culture at Purdue" was a new survey question added in 2013. The percentage of English 620 students who strongly agreed or agreed with the undergraduate roundtable–related statements on this comprehensive course survey increased substantially from fall 2008 to fall 2013 and remained consistently high after 2013, although still not as high as English 620 students' perceptions about the value of having undergraduate volunteers in the audience during their presentations.

The document research in this preliminary, exploratory study indicates that guided by OEPP's mission of supporting ITA candidates by improving their classroom communication skills in ESL, the OEPP volunteer program is mature, structured, and well-integrated into the English 620 course curriculum. In the late 1980s, undergraduate students' negative views of ITA speech comprehensibility were the driving force for the establishment of the OEPP, just like ITA programs on other U.S. university campuses. Interactions with undergraduate students, especially during the simulated teaching presentations, thus, have naturally become an integral part of the ITA training course. Involving undergraduate students—who are an important stakeholder group in the whole ITA scenario—in the teaching presentations strengthens the authenticity and validity of formative classroom assessments involved with simulated teaching presentations. The OEPP volunteers' "written feedback about a grad student's language skills can be one piece of valuable evidence when considering whether to certify the grad student for oral English proficiency or require them to repeat the course" (Kauper, 2019). Likewise, focusing on interactivity and authenticity with less formal and less stressful discussion tasks in the undergraduate "Cookies and Conversation" roundtable provides strong support to the instruction about and practice of interpersonal communication in the English 620 curriculum.

Implications for Policy, Practice, and Future Research

Overall, the OEPP volunteer program is a carefully designed curricular component in the classroom communication course for ITA candidates at Purdue. One advantage of the English 620 presentation-related materials, including the information sheet and evaluation form for undergraduate volunteers, is that these materials are practical and align in terms of evaluation categories and performance levels. The information sheet lists broad categories about presentation skills (e.g., classroom interaction, presence, and delivery) and some recommended expressions that volunteers can use to give suggestions to ITA candidates in the English 620 course. If undergraduate volunteers have time to review this document, they would find it helpful in guiding their commentary on the evaluation form. The five categories in the information sheet line up with the five broad rating criteria on the evaluation form. Combined use of these two documents offers clear guidance to undergraduate audience members on assigning listener scores and providing constructive feedback to the ITA student presenters. In addition, the ITA candidates in the English 620 course were also aware of these volunteer evaluation materials so they could self-assess their presentation during rehearsals. As a matter of fact, the English 620 curriculum includes a presentation self-assessment form that instructors encourage ITA candidates to use to gauge their own performance during rehearsals (Cheng & Kauper, 2010). Therefore, one implication for structured contact programs such as the OEPP undergraduate volunteer program is that evaluation materials, including self-assessment and peer feedback forms, should be developed to align with and complement each other to help reiterate performance criteria to second language learners.

Based on testimonies by the two student representatives and the aggregated reports on the three most recent comprehensive course surveys, it seems that the OEPP volunteer program has received positive feedback from both sides of the linguistic and intercultural interactions, particularly in regards to inviting undergraduate volunteers to observe and evaluate ITA candidates' simulated teaching presentations. Comparatively, there is more data on ITA candidates' perceptions about the value of both types of volunteer activities than there is data on the undergraduate volunteers' perceptions about their volunteering experience. If logistically possible, a future research project and an option for practice could include a quick survey with two or three questions to be administered to the undergraduate volunteers that asks about their volunteering experience and feelings about ITAs before and after volunteering in the English 620 course. The pre-survey could be administered right after a domestic undergraduate student signs up for a volunteer session in the OEPP volunteer program's web application; the post-survey could be incorporated into the evaluation form that the undergraduate volunteer fills out before leaving the English 620 presentation session.

Another implication drawn from this study is that, given institutional support and collaboration with other campus units, structured contact components integrated into an ESL support program, such as the OEPP volunteer activities, can be utilized to strengthen the university's internationalization by integrating an IaH component. Providing ESL language and cultural support is an essential part of the internationalization abroad process for international students; however, the addition of one or more purposely designed curricular activities involving domestic students would help to broaden the base and amplify the positive effects of the university's internationalization efforts. The OEPP volunteer activities are a prime example of one way that domestic undergraduate students can engage in some type of internationalization without leaving the university campus. Through socio-academic and intercultural interactions with international graduate students, domestic undergraduate students contribute to ITA candidates' ESL language development and a university's internationalization abroad goals while simultaneously improving their own international knowledge, skills, and attitudes. Domestic undergraduate students' volunteering experiences are good avenues for IaH, which aims to develop all students' employability skills by immersing them in international and intercultural experiences in a domestic context (Beelen & Jones, 2015, p. 68).

At the operation level, while international programs on a U.S. university campus can develop strategic initiatives to connect domestic and international students, ESL programs can also reach out to other campus units and start with piloting a structured curricular component before gradually scaling it up. Identifying a potential collaborator can be part of the first step: for example, the PLaCE LPP initially identified two Chinese language courses as the source of language partners for the international ESL undergraduates in the PLaCE program. In addition, effective use of technologies can facilitate language and cultural exchange in unusual circumstances. During the 2020–2021 academic year, the COVID-19 pandemic posed unprecedented challenges to international travel, language instruction and assessment, as well as cultural adaptation. However, the OEPP undergraduate volunteer program was not negatively impacted, especially in the presentation observation volunteering sessions. The continued success of the OEPP volunteer program during the pandemic year was attributable to effective use of video conferencing technologies and the OEPP volunteer coordinator's consistent efforts at recruiting domestic undergraduate volunteers.

In conclusion, a carefully designed curricular component embedded into an existing ESL program, such as the OEPP volunteer activities, provides a good answer to Jones' (2013) call for "further exploration of the domestic intercultural context as a vehicle for the kind of transformational learning" for all students (p. 8).

REFERENCES

Beelen, J., & Jones, E. (2015). Redefining internationalization at home. In A. Curai, L. Matei, R. Pricopie, J. Salmi, & P. Scott (Eds.), *The European higher education area: Between critical reflections and future policies* (pp. 67–80). Cham, Switzerland: Springer.

Cheng, L., & Kauper, N. (2010). Using self-assessment for teaching and learning classroom presentation skills. *INTESOL Journal, 7*(1), 25–42.

Haan, J. (2009). *ESL and internationalization at Purdue University: A history and analysis.* Unpublished PhD diss., Purdue University, Indiana.

Jones, E. (2013). Internationalization and employability: The role of intercultural experiences in the development of transferable skills. *Public Money and Management, 33*(2), 95–104.

Kauper, N. L. (2019, March 6). Re: *Involvement of undergraduates in cross-training ITA programs* [listserv post].

Knight, J. (2003). Updated definition of internationalization. *International Higher Education,* (33), https://doi.org/10.6017/ihe.2003.33.7391

Long, M. H. (1996). The role of the linguistic environment in second language acquisition. In W. C. Ritchie & T. K. Bhatia (Eds.), *Handbook of research on language acquisition* (Vol. 2, pp. 413–468). New York: Academic Press.

Neubert, A. P. (2015, November 16). Purdue ranks 3rd for largest international student population at public universities. *Purdue University News.* Retrieved from https://www.purdue.edu/newsroom/releases/2015/Q4/purdue-ranks-3rd-for-largest-international-student-population-at-public-universities.html

OEPP. (2016). FA15+FA13+FA08 ENGL 620 Student Surveys LIKERT comparisons.

OEPP. (2019, September 4). *Volunteer opportunities for undergraduates video* [Video]. YouTube. Retrieved from https://www.youtube.com/watch?v=08ZUden3S_0&feature=youtu.be&_ga=2.251327238.1419143734.1599441657-23877879.1594325821

O'Mara, M. (2012). The uses of the foreign student. *Social Science History, 36*(4), 583–615.

Plonsky, L., & Gass, S. M. (2011). Quantitative research methods, study quality and outcomes: The case of interaction research. *Language Learning, 61*(2), 325–366.

Purdue University. (n.d.a). *Purdue ISS enrollment and statistical reports.* Purdue University International Students and Scholars. Retrieved from https://www.purdue.edu/IPPU/ISS/reports.html

Purdue University. (n.d.b). *Welcome to Purdue!* Purdue University International Students and Scholars. Retrieved from https://www.purdue.edu/ippu/iss/

Purdue University. (1918). *Annual register.* West Lafayette, IN: Purdue University.

Purdue University. (1924). *Annual register.* West Lafayette, IN: Purdue University.

Purdue University. (1926). *Course catalog.* West Lafayette, IN: Purdue University.

Purdue University. (1979). *Report on international education and research at Purdue University.* West Lafayette, IN: Purdue University.

Staples, S., Kang, O., & Wittner, E. (2014). Considering interlocutors in university discourse communities: Impacting U.S. undergraduates' perceptions of ITAs through a structured contact program. *English for Specific Purposes, 35*(1), 54–65.

Sutton, F. X. (1971). *Internationalizing higher education: A United States approach.* International Council for Educational Development.

Ziegler, N. (2016). Synchronous computer-mediated communication and interaction: A meta-analysis. *Studies in Second Language Acquisition, 38*(3), 553–586.

APPENDIX 5A Information Sheet and Evaluation Form for Undergraduate Volunteers to Use

Oral English Proficiency Program
ENGL 620 PRESENTATION EVALUATION FORM

Date: _____ Presenter _____

Topic: _____ Evaluator: Undergraduate Volunteer

Students in ENGL 620 practice for presentations to help them become better communicators in English.

Give your opinion of each aspect of their performance and communication.

English 620 students are not allowed to use power point presentations.

		Needs extensive improvement	Needs improvement	Getting close	Good enough to TA	Excellent	COMMENTS
A.	MATERIALS SELECTION AND ORGANIZATION	35	40	45	50	55	
1.	Organization was logical	35	40	45	50	55	
2.	Important points were clearly identified	35	40	45	50	55	
3.	Appropriate amount of information and detail (not too much or too little)	35	40	45	50	55	
4.	Used appropriate examples	35	40	45	50	55	
B.	CLASSROOM INTERACTION						
1.	Kept good eye contact with students	35	40	45	50	55	
2.	Checked for comprehension	35	40	45	50	55	
3.	Asked clear and relevant questions	35	40	45	50	55	
4.	Provided clear, relevant, and brief responses to questions	35	40	45	50	55	
C.	PRESENCE AND DELIVERY						
1.	Appeared comfortable and poised	35	40	45	50	55	
2.	Volume was adequate	35	40	45	50	55	
3.	Speed was OK (not too fast or too slow)	35	40	45	50	55	
D	LANGUAGE						
1.	TA was understandable	35	40	45	50	55	
2.	Rate the following:						
	Pronunciation	35	40	45	50	55	
	Fluency/Pausing	35	40	45	50	55	
	Rhythm/Stress/Intonation	35	40	45	50	55	
	Grammar	35	40	45	50	55	

E. OVERALL IMPRESSION–Comment on the strengths and weaknesses of this presenter's performance and communication.

_____

_____

Updated 5/30/18

Suggestions from Undergraduates for ITAs

1. Slow down and face your audience so we can see your mouth when you are talking.
2. Break down problems in steps so we can easily understand them. In other words, explain things step-by-step so we get it.
3. We will be patient with you as an international student if you are patient with us when we ask you to repeat things, or explain something again.
4. Project your voice so we can hear it in the back of the room. Do not be afraid to speak up because of your English.
5. Write things on the board to help us understand.
6. Tell us about yourself. We want to get to know you and to hear some stories about your country.
7. Be friendly and build rapport with us. If you see us on campus, say hello!
8. Constant reminders are ver y good about homework assignments.
9. Please post stuff on Blackboard so we can check that.
10. Be open to questions. Do not get angry when we ask questions.
11. "Read" your students' faces. If we are staring blankly at you, we probably do not understand what you are trying to teach us.
12. Check frequently with us to see if we understand. If we don't say no, but just still stare blankly, we probably do not understand.
13. When we email you, please reply promptly.
14. If you are teaching a recitation session, please connect the recitation session to the lecture.
15. Go over homework with us, don't just ask us to hand it in.
16. Remember to repeat the question before answering so we can hear you in the back of the room.
17. Be prepared for your class.
18. Show that you want to teach and a re motivated to do so.
19. Do not do stuff on your cell phone when we want to ask questions in a lab session.
20. Do not speak Chinese when answering Chinese students in class. We cannot understand Chinese, and it is a waste of our time.
21. Please make sure that y ou understand our question before answering it.
22. We would never tell you that you are pronouncing a word incorrectly unless we have your permission to do so.

Part II

Internationalizing Composition

6

Responding to the University's Internationalization: Establishing Placement Mechanisms for Cross-Cultural Composition

Tanita Saenkhum and Hannah Soblo

> I just think that [cross-cultural composition] was really helpful not only on the academic side of it, but also the personal side. It's really good for international and native students to collaborate. [People] say that a lot, but as an international student I don't really see that a lot around campus.
>
> —*Claire (first-year student, originally from South Korea)*

> Growing up, I didn't come from a very diverse hometown. It was mostly Caucasian people and obviously I'm not Caucasian. So coming into a classroom where I saw other people from different backgrounds, it was really encouraging. I enjoyed it a lot.
>
> —*Kayla (first-year student, originally from the United States)*

Claire's and Kayla's (pseudonyms) perceptions as international and domestic students, respectively, demonstrate that it is essential to support university internationalization through a curriculum that provides opportunities for meaningful interactions between students from different backgrounds. As internationalization has become an integral

123

part of U.S. higher education, the increasing diversity of home campuses at U.S. universities (e.g., de Wit & Hunter, 2015; Rose & Weiser, 2018; Siczek, 2018) creates opportunities for all students—whether labeled international or domestic—to gain meaningful learning experiences. In the context of college composition programs, we as administrators see supporting and preparing all student writers to participate in an increasingly internationalized and globalized world as key for writing program administration work.

As a response to our university's internationalization, we (Tanita as the director of L2 Writing and Hannah as assistant director) developed a cross-cultural composition course as a placement option for first-year students. It enrolls an equal number of students whose first or strongest language is English (L1 English speakers) and those whose first or strongest language is not English (L2 English speakers). The course is taught by an instructor who is trained to address the differing needs of diverse groups of students. This placement option, as suggested by seminal research (Matsuda & Silva, 1999; Reichelt & Silva, 1995; Silva, 1994), is intended to provide support and opportunities for all students to develop their intercultural communication skills through meaningful interactions in a multicultural and multilingual environment. Since those 1990s studies, little research has been done on cross-cultural composition, mainly because offering such courses poses administrative challenges, including staffing, scheduling, and budget issues (see Silva, 1994, for a nuanced discussion). However, this chapter (as well as those by Gherwash and Ene & Cohen, this volume) provides a more recent discussion of cross-cultural composition courses as a valuable means of promoting internationalization at home through intentional integration of students from diverse backgrounds.

Our response to internationalization is consistent with recommendations from the Conference on College Composition and Communication (CCCC), which urges writing program administrators (WPAs) and writing teachers to "recognize and take responsibility for the regular presence of multilingual students in writing classes, to understand their characteristics, and to develop instructional and administrative practices that are sensitive to their linguistic and cultural backgrounds" (CCCC Statement on Second Language Writing and Multilingual Writers, 2020, para. 7). As we developed the course, we simultaneously conducted programmatic research to assess its effectiveness as a placement option that can provide support for all students as their university becomes increasingly internationalized.

This chapter, which draws on preliminary results of our research, explores the connection between internationalization and placement, focusing on how we developed and implemented placement procedures that could support internationalization at home (Bathurst & La Brack, 2012; Bennett, 2012; Lantz-Deaton, 2017; Vande Berg, Paige, & Lou, 2012). The goal is to demonstrate that placement mechanisms are essential for courses like cross-cultural composition to succeed. The issues and challenges stemming from the university's internationalization efforts and the institutional context in which we situate the cross-cultural composition curriculum in campus-wide services are discussed first. Then placement mechanisms, including cross-cultural composition design and development and curriculum assessment through student and instructor perceptions, are addressed. Key components to developing and maintaining cross-cultural composition as a placement option are outlined, followed by recommendations for ways that writing programs can support internationalization at home (IaH).

Issues and Challenges Stemming from Internationalization

Our institution, University of Tennessee, Knoxville (UTK), has made serving international students, including undergraduate and graduate students, a priority. According to a database from the Office of Institutional Research and Assessment (K. Wagoner, personal communication, February 19, 2020), between 2010 and 2019 UTK has enrolled on average 27,905 students per year, including 21,815 undergraduate students. About 1.7 percent of the undergraduate students enrolled are international. This data also indicates that, during those ten years, the small enrollment number of international undergraduate students has remained steady (international enrollment during the academic year 2020–21 shrank due to the impact of the global pandemic). UTK has also served a growing body of diverse second language students who are permanent residents and U.S. citizens, but the institution does not keep a record of these students.

In the interest of bringing more international students to campus, especially undergraduates, UTK's International Recruitment Program proposed that the Office of Undergraduate Admissions update admissions criteria by adding ways for international students to demonstrate their English proficiency. These included providing proof of citizenship in a country or a transcript from a high school or university where English was an official language or language of instruction ("Demonstrate English Proficiency," n.d.). These criteria were effective beginning fall 2019. They were added to the existing requirements, such as receiving a required standardized testing score or completing a core intensive curriculum, plus a recommendation from faculty in the university's intensive English program. Tanita, who was director of L2 Writing from August 2013–July 2019, was part of this conversation and was asked by the International Recruitment program to review a list of official English language nations and provide recommendations for countries to omit. These additional criteria for demonstrating English proficiency meant an increase of international undergraduate students on campus. More importantly, it impacted how our L2 Writing Program worked with these students. As WPAs, our goal was to ensure that a placement option, including its curriculum, effectively addressed the writing needs of all student writers regardless of their linguistic and cultural backgrounds.

With this goal in mind, the curriculum of our cross-cultural composition course was designed based on internationalization research, which demonstrates that intercultural competence skills are key for preparing all students for an internationalized world (Bathurst & La Brack, 2012; Bennett, 2012; Vande Berg et al., 2012). By developing this curriculum, we as program directors aimed to achieve the concept of IaH as eloquently described in this volume. Intercultural competence is facilitated through meaningful interactions with peers from different backgrounds, combined with conscious reflections and intervention through an educator or mentor (Bennett, 2012). In these interactions and reflections, cultural differences are explicitly discussed and used to help create meaning that leads to an understanding of students' own culturally specific experiences. Research in this area calls for university policies and administrations to support intercultural communication through educational and policy initiatives, including creating learning opportunities that allow students and teachers to engage in activities or tasks specific to intercultural learning (Byram, 1997; Lantz-Deaton, 2017).

Within the context of IaH, the instructor plays a significant role as a facilitator who uses course content to help students develop their intercultural communication through reflective writings, group assignments, and class discussions with peers from different backgrounds. Through these classroom practices, cross-cultural composition is intended to create opportunities for meaningful interactions across cultures.

Institutional Context

The L2 Writing Program at UTK is part of the Composition Program housed in the English Department. Both programs serve all students across the university. The L2 Writing Program offers a variety of placement options for first-year composition courses, with two main tracks: mainstream and L2 writing. Each track has different levels of first-year writing courses for students to choose from. For the mainstream track, the Composition Program offers the two-semester, first-year writing sequence (English 101 and 102). For the L2 writing track, we offer a developmental writing course (English 121), the two-semester, first-year writing sequence (English 131 and 132), which is equivalent to English 101 and 102, and the cross-cultural composition course (cross-listed English 102/132).

We place L2 undergraduate students into first-year composition courses using a combination of standardized test scores (TOEFL®, IELTS®, SAT®, and ACT®) and an optional in-house placement exam. Students may take the in-house placement exam if they are not satisfied with their placement based on their standardized test scores. The in-house placement exam, which is administered twice a year (fall and spring semesters), consists of reading and writing sections that test students' reading comprehension and writing skills. Readings and designed writing prompts were purposefully selected based on the readings and writing assignments that were similar to those assigned in our first-year writing courses. Students will first read an assigned reading, then answer some specific questions and write a brief timed essay (a minimum of 250 words) based on the assigned reading. Students' placement exams are assessed by our L2 writing instructors, including lecturers and graduate teaching assistants. Rubrics are used to assess written essays. Students cannot retake the placement exam. Through these placement procedures (the combination of standardized test scores and an optional placement exam) for the first-semester writing course, incoming L2 students are placed into either mainstream composition (English 101), L2 writing (English 121 or English 131), or English Language Institute (ELI 110). ELI 110 is a foundational English course taught by the English Language Institute, which is the university's intensive English program and not part of the English department.

Our cross-cultural composition course (English 102/132) is designed as a second-semester writing course. Before we implemented this placement option, a similar course was offered in response to low enrollment numbers in English 132; this course mixed L1 and L2 students into one section aiming to help international students complete the first-year writing requirement on time. When we developed the cross-cultural composition course, we carefully considered three related issues: course sequence, course cap, and enrollment. We chose to offer it as a second-semester course because we believed students would be more mature after becoming familiar with college writing in English 101 or 131. Additionally, the curriculum of the second-semester writing course is more flexible (detailed later), which allowed us to develop our cross-cultural composition in a way that provided students opportunities for intercultural communication.

In addition to the course sequence, we also considered the course cap and enrollment numbers. The course cap of cross-cultural composition is 20; each section enrolls a roughly equal number of L1 (10) and L2 (10) students. Our course cap aligns with recommendations from the CCCC Statement on Second Language Writing and Multilingual Writers (2020) in that it allows instructors to spend more time working with individual students. To ensure equal numbers of the two groups of students in the same class, we have worked closely with our department's associate head and administrative staff who take care of scheduling and course enrollments. For example, we had each group of students sign up separately for either English 102 or English 132, respectively, with our administrative staff helping to monitor enrollment numbers of each cross-listed section.

Responding to the University's Internationalization

Our placement mechanisms began with formalizing the course as a placement option and simultaneously developing the curriculum, followed by ongoing assessment of the curriculum's effectiveness. Through our assessment, we were able to identify benefits and challenges of the course. This discussion draws from the preliminary findings from our larger assessment study, which was conducted during the first four consecutive semesters of the course being offered (spring 2018, fall 2018, spring 2019, and fall 2019).

Formalizing Cross-Cultural Composition as a Placement Option

The process of formalizing cross-cultural composition began in fall 2017 with formal discussions with other departmental administrators and teacher training. Tanita informed the administrators who handle the department's course offerings and first-year composition that the L2 Writing Program wanted to formalize cross-cultural composition as a placement option and was in the process of developing its curriculum to implement it in spring 2018.

Course development took place in the same semester in a graduate course focused on teaching L2 writing taught by Tanita. The course covers various instructional and practical strategies, including course and assignment designs, teacher and peer response, classroom assessment, and error treatment. It enrolls students who are interested in teaching

L2 writing in different contexts and settings, including graduate teaching associates (GTAs). During this course, Tanita had conversations with two GTAs, including Hannah, who specialized in L2 writing, and asked if they would be interested in teaching sections of cross-cultural composition in spring 2018. Both of them wanted to pursue their teaching of L2 writing, and they decided to take on this opportunity. During this course, they worked closely with Tanita to develop their teaching materials, including writing assignments, scaffolding activities, and syllabi to be used in their own classes. The curriculum for cross-cultural composition will be discussed here to give an overview before we use Hannah's curriculum development as a specific example.

Like other sections of the second-semester first-year writing requirement (English 102 and English 132), cross-cultural composition had to follow the Composition Program's standardized curriculum: classes must be research-based and include three research projects—secondary source, archival, and qualitative—centered on a theme of the instructor's choosing. We encourage instructors of cross-cultural composition to choose themes that are accessible to diverse students. Three of the successful themes for cross-cultural composition sections have been inquiry into cross-cultural identities, inquiry into genre, and inquiry into food as a cultural practice.

The theme for Hannah's two sections, which are the focus of this chapter, was inquiry into cross-cultural identities, which explicitly focused on the nature and development of cross-cultural communication. The purpose of this theme was to integrate means of developing students' intercultural competence into the research-based writing curriculum through discussion of and reflections on cross-cultural interactions, which was identified as important for the success of cross-cultural composition by Matsuda and Silva (1999; see also Silva, 1994). To enable students to develop their intercultural communication skills, the three major research assignments asked students to investigate issues related to place, language, and identity. Students' research topics included representations of people and places in tourist media, the ways academic research has treated marginalized populations, and qualitative interview studies in which they spoke with peers about their practices of academic literacy. Scaffolding activities were also emphasized, including reflective writings, class discussions, and peer review. Hannah took class time to provide instruction for students on how to productively collaborate on writing projects, culminating in a final research project that was done in groups of two or three.

While Hannah was developing her course materials, we promoted cross-cultural composition courses among our first-year composition instructors via the Composition Program's listserv and asked the instructors to share this information with their current students who were taking their first-semester, first-year composition courses. Our promotional email included relevant course-related information, including what the course was about, its benefits, and how students could register for the course.

Ongoing Assessment: Benefits and Challenges Identified and Our Response

To assess the effectiveness of our cross-cultural composition as a placement option, we conducted programmatic assessment research that collected data through interviews with students, instructors, and the program director. We began collecting this data after the spring 2018 semester of English 102/132. As we conducted interviews with students from Hannah's two sections, we had regular formal discussions with each other as co-researchers and WPAs to identify challenges and how these might be addressed in subsequent semesters. The student interviews and our periodic discussions allowed us to gain a better perspective on what had worked well, what challenges had occurred, and how we might modify any of our approaches to improve the course. We continued this process of data collection in the next three semesters through fall 2019. In total, we conducted interviews with 15 students and four instructors, as well as with the WPA (Tanita).

During the four consecutive semesters of data collection (spring 2018, fall 2018, spring 2019, fall 2019), our course development followed an iterative process of data collection, assessment, and adjustments or alterations made to the next semester's sections. Through our programmatic assessment research, we have gained a better understanding from students and instructors about the benefits of cross-cultural composition as a placement option. Concurrently, we were able to identify several initial challenges and subsequently address them.

Benefits of Cross-Cultural Composition

Drawing on student interviews, we were able to identify several key benefits of cross-cultural composition. These included providing a more diverse classroom and campus environment and practicing communication skills that students found beneficial to their futures beyond the classroom (all student names included are pseudonyms).

Student participants reported that they found the cross-cultural composition classroom to be a valuable space to engage in meaningful interactions while at the home campus. They also felt that there was a general lack of such opportunities for interactions at the university. A comment from an L1 English-speaking student, Kayla, summarizes these views: "I would 100 percent do it again if they offer something similar to this. I just don't know of any other class that specifically is cross-cultural. . . . I think everyone should at one point take a class similar to this." Other students shared Kayla's perceptions of the need for more opportunities for intercultural communication, such as Claire (quoted at the beginning of the chapter). Their comments demonstrated the value of this course as a way of introducing L1 students to intercultural communication. Student comments also addressed the benefits of the curriculum, such as classroom discussions that were more interesting due to the diversity of perspectives. Hailey, who self-identified as an L2 speaker of English, described the benefits of having students from different backgrounds in this way: "Since we're all from different backgrounds and different countries, then I think it's more dynamic in terms of discussing some stuff, because we have different perspectives and there's gonna be more different ideas." Other students, from a variety of language backgrounds, reported similar interests in both classroom discussions as well as research presentations from peers who introduced them to perspectives they had not considered previously.

Students also felt that, beyond the immediate campus context, learning how to understand others and collaborate through or in spite of cultural and/or communicative differences was a valuable skill that would be important to their futures. For instance, students found it helpful to use language skills that they otherwise would not have had the opportunity to practice. Mark, an L1 student, explained that his partnership with a native Mandarin speaker was helpful for both of their language learning goals: "It's beneficial for both of us because he's from China and I'll speak English with him, help him with that, and he helps me with Mandarin." This view of the benefit of having a space to practice L2 language skills was shared by both international and L1 students. Students also found the course helpful to overcome their nervousness over interacting with people from different backgrounds, which would help prepare them for future internationalized careers. An international student gave a typical account of these experiences: "[It] was very helpful for everybody to appreciate each other, respect each other, and know each other's culture and how we engage in society." Other L1 students reported similar experiences, and several mentioned that gaining experience in intercultural communication would be valuable preparation for study abroad or international career goals in the future. As a whole, these students' perceptions confirm the need for curricular responses like cross-cultural composition to internationalization that provide students opportunities to practice intercultural communication skills.

Challenges of Implementing Cross-Cultural Composition for Placement

Although there were many benefits of cross-cultural composition as identified by students, there were also challenges to learning to collaborate across linguistic or cultural differences. These challenges, which were identified by both the instructor and student interviewees, were compounded when students did not realize that they were signing up for a cross-cultural composition section of English 102. The majority of student participants revealed that they registered for the course because it fit their schedule without knowing that it had a cross-cultural focus. Instructor interviewees also reported noticing the presence of students who were unaware that they were enrolled in a cross-listed section and noted that these students could be problematic to the learning environment. For example, one instructor said that a student in their English

102 who had not realized that the course was cross-listed with a section of English 132 "told me outright in [their] reflective responses and in person once or twice that [they] did not want to be put in a group with international students, [they] felt like . . . [they] just couldn't work with [international students]." While most students were receptive to encountering and engaging with differences and felt the course overall was a positive experience, some students (like the one described) were unable to overcome their preconceived notions about international students during the course.

Responding to the Challenges

After learning from the interviews with students and teachers that students did not receive sufficient information about cross-cultural composition as a placement option, we refined how we communicated that information to related stakeholders, including students, academic advisors, and instructors. Initially, when we implemented cross-cultural composition in spring 2018, we only promoted the course among our first-year composition instructors. Placement research by Saenkhum (2016, p. 112) has demonstrated that making "complete and accurate placement information" available to students is essential for them to make well-informed placement decisions. Guided by her research, we reached out to each stakeholder group using different strategies.

For our outreach to students, we created a brochure that included information about the course section numbers, themes, and times offered, as well as why the course could be valuable to them. We posted copies of the printed brochure in areas frequented by students, such as the English department office building, the buildings where most English courses were held, and at the International House, which is an informal gathering place for international students where they can find resources and support provided by the university. We also learned from interviews with students and instructors that, during the spring and fall 2019 semesters, students began hearing about the course option from friends who had previously taken the course. For instructors, we sent digital copies of the brochure along with an overview of the course that they could use to introduce it to students enrolled in English 101 or

131. For academic advisors, Tanita sent directors of academic advising an informational email detailing English 102/132 as a placement option and how the course could benefit all student writers, and she asked them to share this information with their students.

Our placement communication efforts paid off. After three consecutive semesters of the course being offered, there was improvement of student placement through our outreach. During the spring and fall 2019 semesters, instructor interviewees reported that most students who enrolled in their cross-cultural composition courses were aware of and excited about the fact that it was cross-listed. These students were also interested in a cross-cultural focus. To illustrate, student awareness was demonstrated most clearly by one instructor who taught sections of cross-cultural composition in spring 2019. He brought up that the course attracted U.S. resident students who were first- and second-generation immigrant students. This differed from previous years; several previous instructors reported that many of their domestic students were unaware that it was cross-cultural composition. This included Hannah, who explained in the interview with the spring 2019 instructor that his experience differed significantly from her own. In contrast, she said: "The majority of my students [in spring 2018] had no idea. I had some students come up to me after the class on the first day and be like, I'm not sure, am I in the right room?"

In short, we improved our placement communication through outreach to multiple stakeholders, including not only instructors but also students and academic advisors. By getting the word out about the course, students were fully informed of how it differed from a traditional section of English 102 or English 132, and students who were interested in the course would sign up. By communicating cross-cultural composition as a placement option to related stakeholders, we were able to encourage the presence of students who were interested in cross-cultural experiences and in gaining intercultural communication skills.

By establishing the placement mechanisms discussed, our L2 Writing Program is now able to consistently offer cross-cultural composition as a placement option. We would therefore argue that well-established placement mechanisms are one important component that can enable institutions to support courses designated for IaH, helping such courses to succeed.

Discussion

Having shown how cross-cultural composition as a placement option can be a local curricular response to internationalization at the university, we now consider several key components that can help other writing programs establish their placement mechanisms that support and maintain cross-cultural composition.

Collaboration with Other Departmental Administrators

For writing program administrators interested in developing cross-cultural composition, the first step is to have a conversation with other departmental administrators who are involved in curriculum development, course registration, budgeting, undergraduate recruitment, and teacher recruitment/preparation. Then it is essential to write a proposal that details: the purpose of the course, its benefits to students and other stakeholders, how the course will be staffed and scheduled, and any budget requirements. The proposal should also explain how the course can provide support for all student writers regardless of cultural and linguistic backgrounds in developing intercultural competence and offer opportunities for guided instruction and intentional collaboration in cross-cultural contexts. To advocate for the course, WPAs can draw on results from current cross-cultural composition research, such as ours (or that described in Ene & Cohen, this volume), as well as connect the proposal to their university's mission statement for internationalization, if there is one. Doing so will enable WPAs to situate the course within the larger university. To maintain the course as a placement option, WPAs should work closely with their departments to determine: how many sections will be offered each semester, how these sections will be staffed, and who will monitor course enrollments of each cross-listed section. This discussion needs to take place every semester to ensure that cross-cultural composition courses are offered regularly. Since transitions of administrative roles are inevitable, current WPAs should keep incoming WPAs informed. In our case, the L2 Writing Program transitioned to an interim director in summer 2019.

Teacher Training and Preparation

Teacher training is another important component, since cross-cultural composition requires teachers who are trained to address the differing needs of diverse students in the same class. WPAs should provide training avenues, teaching resources, and opportunities for ongoing support for both graduate students and lecturers. These can come in various forms, including formal classroom visits or informal teaching discussions. For graduate students, graduate-level courses like the one offered at our institution should be offered regularly. Such courses allow prospective teachers to develop their skills and materials and to establish a community of L2 writing teachers. For institutions without the resources for a formal course, or for lecturers who may not have the time for a full semester training course, WPAs can offer workshops that focus on teaching writing to diverse students, with workshop leaders either from their own institution or by inviting outside L2 writing specialists. Both coursework and workshops can contribute to forming a community in which teachers discuss classroom practices and share teaching materials. After the training course or workshop, ongoing support should be made available to teachers.

In our context, we found that, as more teachers taught the course, an informal community of L2 writing teachers developed, with former instructors mentoring current instructors by offering advice and sharing course assignments. We continued to offer informal teaching discussions to current instructors, classroom observations, and other teaching resources. However, as more instructors became certified and taught the course, less effort was required from us as WPAs to help new instructors negotiate classroom challenges or develop course materials. Instead, the community has allowed instructors to assist one another. Since the end of data collection in fall 2019, at least two sections of the cross-cultural composition course have been offered in every semester through spring 2021, and there are plans for the course to continue in the future. A total of six GTAs and two lecturers have taught the course in the semesters from spring 2018 through spring 2021, and we will continue recruiting GTAs in the future through Tanita's graduate course on teaching L2 writing.

Outreach to Students

Obviously, for the course to succeed, information about the cross-cultural composition course should be made available to students. This information should include how the course differs from other courses, what the benefits are, and why students might be interested in taking it. WPAs can make this information available to students through multiple avenues, including disseminating information through academic advisors and instructors of earlier prerequisite courses. Student outreach should also be done directly through printed materials like brochures. These outreach efforts should be concentrated in the first few semesters the course is offered. Based on our experience, when the course is offered consistently, awareness will spread as students begin to tell each other about the course.

Since our programmatic assessment study ended in fall 2019, we have been able to offer the course consistently, even once the program transferred to an interim director. We have been able to maintain the course as a placement option by keeping an open dialogue with the current interim director; advertising the course to students, instructors, and academic advisors (our earlier efforts); and establishing a community of teachers.

Closing Thoughts

By establishing our placement mechanisms for cross-cultural composition and its assessment as a placement option, we sought to provide an opportunity for intentionally integrating L1 and L2 students to support IaH efforts. Our assessment taught us that cross-cultural composition promotes IaH by helping students improve the oral and written communication skills necessary to interact in a globalizing world. Our students valued these skills and viewed the course as helpful both in their learning and preparations for future careers as part of a diverse/global workforce. At the programmatic level, we learned that placement mechanisms, including development and assessment of the cross-cultural composition course as a placement option, are essential for our program to consistently offer the course. In the future, we hope to offer more sections to continue to further internationalization on our campus.

Based on our assessment, offering cross-cultural composition as a second-semester writing course is appropriate in our local context. However, other writing programs may consider offering it as a first-semester writing course if it addresses their local needs better. Regardless of the sequence, writing programs should establish placement mechanisms that allow courses like cross-cultural composition to be offered regularly and continually assess their placement mechanisms by learning from students and instructors. In our context, we will continue to assess whether our placement mechanisms promote internationalization and prepare students for an internationalized world.

REFERENCES

Bathurst, L., & La Brack, B. (2012). Shifting the locus of intercultural learning: Intervening prior to and after student experiences abroad. In M. V. Berg, R. M. Paige, & K. H. Lou (Eds.), *Student learning abroad: What our students are learning, what they're not, and what we can do about it* (pp. 261–284). Sterling, VA: Stylus.

Bennett, M. J. (2012). Paradigmatic assumptions and a developmental approach to intercultural learning. In M. V. Berg, R. M. Paige, & K. H. Lou (Eds.), *Student learning abroad: What our students are learning, what they're not, and what we can do about it* (pp. 90–115). Sterling, VA: Stylus.

Byram, M. (1997). *Teaching and assessing intercultural communicative competence*. New York: Multilingual Matters.

CCCC Statement on Second Language Writing and Multilingual Writers (2020). Retrieved from https://cccc.ncte.org/cccc/resources/positions/secondlangwriting

"Demonstrate English Proficiency." (n.d.). Retrieved from https://admissions.utk.edu/apply/international-students/

de Wit, H., & Hunter, F. (2015). The future of internationalization of higher education in Europe. *International Higher Education, 83*, 2–3. https://doi.org/10.6017/ihe.2015.83.9073

Lantz-Deaton, C. (2017). Internationalisation and the development of students' intercultural competence. *Teaching in Higher Education, 22*(5), 532–550.

Matsuda, P. K., & Silva, T. (1999). Cross-Cultural composition: Mediated integration of US and international students. *Composition Studies, 27*(1), 15–30.

Reichelt, M., & Silva, T. (1995). Cross-Cultural composition. *TESOL Journal, 5*(2), 16–19.

Rose, S.K. & Weiser, I. (Eds.). (2018). *The internationalization of U.S. writing programs.* Louisville: University Press of Colorado/Utah State University Press. doi: 10.7330/9781607326762.c000

Saenkhum, T. (2016). *Decisions, agency, and advising: Key issues in the placement of multilingual writers into first-year composition courses.* Logan: Utah State University Press.

Siczek, M. (2018). *International students in first-year writing: A journey through socio-academic space.* Ann Arbor: University of Michigan Press.

Silva, T. (1994). An examination of writing program administrators' options for the placement of ESL students in first-year writing classes. *Writing Program Administration, 18*(1–2), 37–43.

Vande Berg, M., Paige, R. M., & Lou, K. H. (2012). Student learning abroad: Paradigms and assumptions. In M. V. Berg, R. M. Paige, & K. H. Lou (Eds.), *Student learning abroad: What our students are learning, what they're not, and what we can do about it* (pp. 3–29). Sterling, VA: Stylus.

7

Internationalized First-Year Writing by Design

Estela Ene and Mary Ann Cohen

The concept of internationalization at home (IaH) was introduced in 2001 by Crowther and colleagues in a position paper for the European Association for International Education to advocate for working to bring the benefits of internationalization to all students rather than only the few who can partake in study abroad. IaH can be achieved in a number of ways, including through increased engagement between domestic and international students through an internationalized curriculum that is guided by global learning goals that are often articulated at institutional levels (Knight, 2006; Leask, 2009). IaH promotes deeper cultural understanding among domestic and international students, for the benefit of all; additionally, it helps offset the inequities inherent to internationalizing only through costly study abroad (Miles, 2018).

Little has been written about how writing courses can contribute to the advancement of IaH, but this has started to change. Siczek and Shapiro (2014) signaled that collaborations between TESOL and writing program specialists are necessary to create internationalized writing curricula and a more inclusive climate that values the international diversity on our campuses. Similarly, in the introduction to their collection *The Internationalization of U.S. Writing Programs,* Weiser and Rose (2018) showed that writing faculty and program administrators "see the new reality of a much more linguistically, culturally, ethnically, geographically diverse student population as a challenging opportunity to review and revise their curriculum and pedagogy, the professional-development opportunities provided to their faculty, and their campus-wide collaborations" (p. 7). Chapters in their book, contributed by scholars in writing studies and applied linguistics (such as Christine Tardy and Susan Miller-Cochran, David Martins and Stan Van Horn, Gail Shuck and Daniel Wilber, Paul Matsuda and Catherine O'Meara), illustrate that "when international and domestic students are enrolled in the same courses, the kind of exposure to language and cultural differences that is an oft-stated reason for internationalizing our campuses benefits both groups of students" (p. 8).

Interactions between domestic and international students not only promote cross-cultural exchange and improved cultural understanding (Andrade, 2006) but also help counteract the isolation of international students from their domestic peers, who often come across as uninterested in international students (Mina & Cimasko, 2020). Existing work, therefore, suggests that internationalized (writing) curricula make the best of multicultural diversity and promote inclusivity (Siczek & Shapiro, 2014).

This chapter adds to the body of literature about internationalized writing curricula by providing an example of cross-program collaboration between an English for Academic Purposes (EAP) program and a writing program (WP) that led to an internationalized first-year writing (FYW) course in which the students developed their cultural awareness together. In internationalized FYW courses, we see opportunities to begin building the open-mindedness, global awareness, and critical-thinking skills needed later in the students' disciplines and careers (Martins & Van Horn, 2018). Because FYW is an early core experience of most students in North American higher education, it provides an ideal site for internationalization.

Internationalized FYW is emerging as one answer to the enduring question of whether and how domestic and international students, or speakers of English as a first (L1) or second (L2)/additional language, can learn successfully together in FYW—and other—college courses. Ideas about this have evolved drastically over time. Before the 1990s, the most common practice was to mainstream students whose L1 was not English to prepare them for the rest of their academic career, in which they would also be mainstreamed. In the 1990s, scholars advocated for separate ESL writing courses designed to meet the unique needs of ESL students (Silva, 1994, p. 39) and where these students would feel more comfortable (Liu, 2001). Another solution proposed during the same period entailed cross-cultural writing courses, also known as multicultural or mixed composition, which drew on the strengths of both populations and segregated neither (Silva, 1994; Matsuda, 2010; Matsuda & Silva, 1999, 2011). The cross-cultural composition option was a predecessor of the translingual view that students' linguistic and cultural diversity is a pedagogical resource rather than a deficit (Canagarajah, 2016). Cross-cultural writing courses were envisioned as courses in which the students would engage in cross-cultural interaction with each other and course readings, assignments, and activities that would bring to the fore perspectives from the students' own cultures and languages. Cross-cultural writing courses were seen as distinct from both ESL and mainstream writing classes by also having teachers trained in both writing and ESL (Matsuda & Silva, 2011), a "more or less equal" mix of L1 and L2 English speakers, and purposeful administrative supervision for this distinct placement option (Silva, 1994).

Unfortunately, research has failed to solidify a distinct place for cross-cultural writing. Few studies describe and analyze the purposeful design and delivery of cross-cultural writing courses which focus on intercultural interaction and communication in the process of teaching writing. An example of such a notable exception is Matsuda and Silva (1999), which showcases how Matsuda, an English as an L2 user trained in writing studies and ESL, used culture-focused assignments, activities, and interactions to facilitate cross-cultural learning for both the ESL and the English as an L1–speaking students. Similarly, a study conducted by Ene and Liu (2003; also Ene & Burrup, 2001) at the University of Arizona found that students and teachers perceived the course positively, and—despite initial reservations—all students ended up finding discussions and peer reviews to be enjoyable and culturally enlightening. The three teachers who taught the cross-cultural course agreed on the importance of knowing how to address the linguistic needs of the ESL writers in addition to navigating cultural diversity and developing intercultural competence for both the domestic and the international students. In the current volume, the chapters by Saenkhum and Soblo and by Gherwash address the administrative process of managing their cross-cultural composition courses in addition to describing their courses and student perceptions about them. Recent research on internationalization supports the idea that multilingual writing courses for international students taught by ESL experts are optimal (Shuck & Wilber, 2018), although student agency in placement is also being advocated (Saenkhum, 2016).

Internationalized writing courses can look different from one another (as can be seen in chapters in Rose & Weiser, 2018) but are motivated by the shared value that writing courses need to prepare students for transnational literacy realities. Starting from this assumption, Martins and Van Horn (2018) showed how a FYW and an EAP director developed internationalized writing courses by building on their strengths as teachers and scholars. Martins' use of literacy narrative/autoethnographic analysis assignments complemented Van Horn's familiarity with intercultural learning, resulting in a writing course with new learning outcomes focused on students understanding language as a resource and a shaping factor (p. 153). After analyzing themes from their students' Writing Literacy Project and the instructors' journals, Martins and Van Horn's concluded:

> We believe internationalizing FYW must extend beyond business as usual focused on topics like World Englishes, the global digital divide, and identity. Our experiences have us focused on (1) designing opportunities for students to interact in socially diverse activities and reflect deeply in writing on their communication experiences and (2) identifying key concepts instructors and students can use to make sense of the complex communication experiences in those contexts. (p. 164)

The course we explore in this chapter implemented the goals and design elements of cross-cultural, internationalized courses—namely, to develop international and domestic students' cultural understanding through a collaboration between experts in two programs that resulted in a deliberate focus on cross-cultural collaboration and reflection. Our analysis focuses on the cultural, linguistic, and writing-related transformations experienced by the students.

Our Context

We created a course for international and domestic students—speakers of English as an L1 and L2/additional language—that focused on global topics (such as elections and immigration) and emphasized their exploration from global perspectives under the guidance of a teacher trained in writing and ESL. We refer to the course we co-designed, and which Cohen taught, as Internationalized Writing, in keeping with the focus of this volume. We refer to our participants as EAP students and WP students, based on their enrollment path into the course.

We created this course at Indiana University–Purdue University Indianapolis (IUPUI), a public, urban university in the Midwest region of the United States. Before the COVID-19 pandemic, the campus enrolled about 20,000 students, of which about 8–10 percent were international, primarily from China, India, and Saudi Arabia. During the pandemic, international student enrollment dropped, mirroring national and international trends. As the world moves past the pandemic, applications may rise from students in some countries, but projected enrollments in the near future are unlikely to reach pre-pandemic levels. Even with fewer international students on campus, internationalized courses will remain an important means to create opportunities for cross-cultural interaction and learning for both international students and their domestic peers. IUPUI designated internationalization as a strategic goal in 2007, and more recently the university has been pursuing internationalization at home (see this volume's introduction). The institution also has a director of curriculum internationalization and has formalized dimensions of global learning for all students (IUPUI, 2020). Many individual courses have been internationalized by faculty across the curriculum.

Both EAP and WP FYW courses have diverse student populations that position them well for internationalization. The students enrolled in the EAP program are primarily international visa students, though some are recent immigrants and refugees who are admitted as domestic students. The WP has some domestic multilingual students, as well as a small number of international students who test out of EAP requirements, in addition to domestic students for whom English is their first language. Thus, some room for student agency (Saenkhum, 2016) exists in FYW placement in that both some international and some domestic students benefit from the option to complete their FYW requirement in either program.

EAP's required, credit-bearing FYW course (G131) is equivalent to the WP's W131. As is more typical of EAP programs, the EAP curriculum and pedagogy are deliberately oriented toward cross-cultural understanding (Martins & Van Horn, 2018). EAP courses bear general education credit for cultural understanding and are designated as internationalized (I) courses. G131 does not carry this credit because it is part of the general education core, but EAP instructors approach the class with the purpose of enhancing cultural understanding.

Both similarities and differences exist between the FYW courses of the EAP and the WP programs in our context. W131: Reading, Writing, and Inquiry is a course that "builds students' abilities to read written and cultural texts critically; to analyze those texts in ways that engage both students' own experiences and the perspectives of others; and to write about those texts for a range of audiences and purposes as a means of participating in broader conversations" (IUPUI, 2018, para. 2). Students produce three to four essays and select which to include as part of a portfolio. EAP's G131 is W131 adapted for EAP—in other words, both courses have the same learning goals; a multi-draft, process-oriented approach to writing; and major writing assignments. G131 instructors provide EAP students with copious feedback on papers, conduct writing conferences, and embed intercultural rhetoric and grammar instruction in the course.

Our Internationalized Writing Course

In fall 2016, we created a FYW course for EAP and WP students that was taught again in fall 2018 and 2019. Distinctive features of the course, including the logistical and pedagogical adaptations, are described.

Logistics: Schedule Advising Notes and Course Caps

A note in the schedule of classes informed students and advisors that W131/G131 was a combined section. The course was set up so that up to two-thirds of the students would be EAP students, based on concerns that they would be intimidated if out-numbered by English L1 students (Liu, 2001).

Designer and Instructor Choice

Based on earlier work on cross-cultural composition (Silva, 1994; Ene & Burrup, 2001; Ene & Liu, 2003; Matsuda & Silva, 1999, 2011), we deemed it important that the instructor for Internationalized Writing should have ESL credentials or experience. Cohen has a TESOL certificate and has been a writing instructor in the WP since 1993 while also teaching off and on for the EAP program since 2008. Ene has been directing the EAP Program at IUPUI since 2009. She teaches and researches EAP writing, provides faculty professional development about writing and intercultural learning on campus, and taught and researched cross-cultural composition at the University of Arizona. The kind of partnership we established to co-design and research internationalized writing represents a cross-program and cross-disciplinary collaboration whose value has been highlighted by others as well (Gherwash, this volume; Martins & Van Horn, 2018; Saenkhum & Soblo, this volume; Shuck & Wilber, 2018; Weiser & Rose, 2018).

Assignments

Autobiographical Narrative

The first paper assigned to the students was an autobiographical narrative, designed to "prompt students from dominant positionalities to reexamine how their worldviews are formed, and how such views impact others relationally, politically, and emotionally" (Yam, 2018, p. 11). We find similarities with Martins and Van Horn's (2018) Writing Literacy Project in an internationalized writing course. In this assignment developed from *The Allyn & Bacon Guide to Writing*, our students were asked to narrate experiences of (1) overcoming an obstacle with language or literacy or (2) educating someone about their culture. Autobiographical narratives are not a required part of the W131/G131 curriculum and, to our knowledge, other instructors do not typically focus on language and culture if they use this type of assignment. Our students needed to explain how the narrated experience conveyed insight (Ramage, Bean, & Johnson, 2006, p.169). They were asked to engage in discussions about the assignment in hopes that they would build a sense of community, arrive at a narrative focus, and become comfortable giving each other feedback. The assignment was also designed to help the students develop confidence about the relevance of their experiences and provide opportunities to present their unique perspectives in future thesis-driven essays. A primary goal of the autobiographical narrative was to foster opportunities for all students to be exposed to and mutually respect differing culturally based perspectives.

Summary Response and Synthesis

The other two writing assignments, as in other W131 and G131 courses, included a summary response in which the students had to respond from a personal perspective to a single source on a topic, and a synthesis paper in which the analysis must contextualize the personal response in a research-based argument. We sequenced the assignments to help students gain confidence expressing and responding to culturally diverse personal perspectives.

Portfolios

In addition to the three above-mentioned papers, the students submitted two portfolios during the course. At the mid-term point, students selected one of their two essays and developed a reflection essay, called a retrospective essay, about how they were working to achieve the course goals. The final portfolio contained two essays (one from the first half of the semester and one from the second) and another retrospective piece. Students also submitted peer reviews and statements analyzing how they revised their work and whether or not they gained cultural awareness.

Student-Chosen Assignment Topics and Readings

Unlike typical FYW courses at our institution, we involved the students in selecting assignment topics based on contemporary socio-political, globally relevant concerns. The students collaboratively chose the course topics through a brainstorming activity in which they discussed current issues that were of interest to themselves and their countries (e.g., election protocols and media coverage, nuclear energy, immigration, same-sex parenting, international adoption). In small- and large-group discussions during this process, the students had to justify why the topics they selected were locally and globally relevant. Students voted on three final selections and then had to find sources that represented different perspectives to use in their papers during the semester. While the majority of FYW course teachers at IUPUI base their essay writing around a non-fiction book or a series of essays, our students selected their topics from Gale's (2020) Opposing Viewpoints database.

Dialogic Activities

To write their essays, the students engaged in oral debates to encounter new perspectives and be challenged to defend perspectives other than their own. The class was divided into two groups, and students took turns being the spokesperson for their group. The groups developed arguments for the side of the issue they were given, whether or not they agreed with it.

Enhanced Peer Review Responses

Compared to other FYW courses, students were asked to take an additional step during the peer review process to focus specifically on the relationship between their writing and their cross-cultural learning experience. In addition to (1) providing feedback to a peer, (2) indicating what revisions they wanted to make, and (3) showing where and how changes were made, students were also instructed by guidelines on the peer review form to also (4) indicate where or how their writing and thinking were changed as a result of the cultural knowledge they gained from giving and receiving feedback from students from a different culture.

Study Design

Although the courses were capped so that two-thirds of the class would be EAP students, scheduling conflicts during the enrollment period did not permit adherence to this plan. Thirty-one EAP and 31 WP students enrolled in the Internationalized Writing course in three fall semesters in 2016 (10 EAP and 12 WP students), 2018 (11 EAP and 10 WP students), and 2019 (10 EAP and 9 WP). The EAP students were international speakers of ESL/EAL, and most of the WP students were U.S. domestic speakers of English as an L1, though a few were domestic multilingual (Generation 1.5) writers. The EAP students came from India, Malaysia, Vietnam, Myanmar, Brazil, Nigeria, Saudi Arabia, Israel, and Venezuela. The majority of the EAP students (65 percent, or 20) had been in the United States and at the university for less than a year, but they had studied English in their home countries for more than ten years.

To gather student perceptions about their achievement of the course goals and how their perspectives and/or writing might have shifted, we used peer review responses, student portfolio retrospectives, and an end-of-semester survey. The survey yielded quantitative results. We performed a qualitative analysis of the students' comments in the peer review responses, as well as the retrospectives.

The course offered in 2016 served as a pilot. We collected end-of-semester surveys and final portfolio retrospectives. The instructor noticed that peer reviews focused predominantly on obvious language and organization issues. To orient the students toward content and the multicultural dimensions of the class, in 2018 and 2019 we added the question "What cultural knowledge did you gain from the assignment or peer review?"

Findings

Themes from Peer Review Responses

Responses to the Autobiographical Narrative

Thirty students completed peer review responses for the autobiographical narrative. Of these, 10 EAP (33 percent) and 13 WP (43 percent) students addressed the culture question. The students worked in pairs, conducting more than one review, and voluntarily interacted across the EAP and WP groups more than within.

We first divided the 23 answers based on the topics they referred to, obtaining 28 comments. The themes that emerged from grouping the topics were about understanding culture, language, and writing norms (as shown in Table 7.1).

Most of the comments (64.3 percent) referred to the students' developing their cultural understanding. Students perceived two main reasons why they gained a better understanding of their own and others' cultures in the Internationalized Writing courses: (1) they had the opportunity to learn something new, and (2) they became aware

TABLE 7.1: Areas in Which the Students in the Internationalized Course Developed

Student Group	Understanding Culture		Understanding Language		Understanding Writing Norms		
	Number of Comments	Percentage from Total Number of Comments (28)	Number of Comments	Percentage from Total Number of Comments (28)	Number of Comments	Percentage from Total Number of Comments (28)	Total Number of Comments
EAP	7	25%	2	7.1%	3	10.7%	12
WP	11	39.3%	4	14.3%	1	3.6%	16
EAP+WP	18	64.3%	6	21.4%	4	14.3%	28

of different perspectives. Students reported learning about the values, norms, and practices of other societies. WP students reflected on the role of place, religion, race, and social norms in defining one's identity and sense of belonging, as illustrated in the comments we will share under pseudonym-based initials.

- ○ "I learned that culture doesn't have to be a way of religion or race, but where you come from. I come from a small town; my culture involves me knowing everyone and feeling out of place when in a room full of strangers." (JE, WP, 2019)
- ○ "Writing this paper helped remind me of how the smallest morals of a different culture can make one feel so unwelcome. It makes me wonder if Americans do anything that makes people with different ethnic backgrounds feel unwelcome." (JO, WP, 2018)

In the language-related answers (21.4 percent of the total), one EAP student sounded empowered as he "remembered that English is not everyone's first language," and a WP student reached a higher level of understanding about the impact of accents:

- ○ "I used to think that my accent held me back from fully communicating my ideas. I found out that there are other ways in which people feel held back or subdued." (CH, WP, 2018)

After interacting with a multilingual WP student, one EAP student (AM) tried to imagine what it would be like not to speak one's own mother tongue fluently. His empathy for his classmate pushed him to be more introspective about the relationships among language, culture, and identity.

Finally, some students gained awareness of how writing norms differ across languages and cultures:

- ○ "The structuring of paragraphs and language styles are different from what I learnt in my system of education, which was mainly British based." (AM, EAP, 2018)

Responses on the Summary Response

For the peer review response related to the summary response assignment, 18 students (55 percent, 11 EAP and 7 WP) of 33 who completed the peer review addressed the question about cultural knowledge gained.

The students' answers were more focused and detailed but less thematically varied than in the peer review response for the autobiographical narrative. We obtained 18 mono-thematic answers from 18 students. As in the case of the autobiographical narrative, the dominant theme had to do with understanding culture. Ten students (55 percent) reported gaining factual knowledge or adjusting their views after being exposed to arguments from another cultural perspective. For example:

- ○ "Different people of different cultures handle issues differently; my peer wrote a paper on euthanasia which is a heavily debated topic here but back in my home country I don't recall people discussing this at all." (AM, EAP, 2018)
- ○ "I read through a paper that I may not have completely agreed with, but I saw their side of it." (LI, WP, 2018)

Answers about writing norms were the second most frequent (8, or 44 percent), with 6 by EAP students who reflected on learning how to write persuasively by U.S. academic norms. Some WP students realized that writing strategies differ across cultures: "I've learned that some people have a different writing style than my own" (KI, WP, 2018).

All in all, the peer review responses revealed evidence of increased cultural (self-)understanding and flexibility among both the EAP and the WP students. This included increased awareness of language-identity connections as well as linguistic/writing conventions.

Themes from the Retrospective Essays

In the retrospective essays submitted with the final portfolio, students were encouraged to reflect on how they and their writing had been influenced in the internationalized course. Thirty-one (53 percent) of the 58 students who completed the retrospective—18 EAP and 13 WP students—offered comments related to this prompt. Students described growing as writers, both in skill and in confidence. For example:

○ "English W131/G131 . . . is not only where I learn to develop my writing skills but also where I communicate my ideas about different topics with international students as well as native English speakers. . . . I had doubts about my ability to develop this skill and therefore I had been feeling unconfident with my writing until I took this class. The fact that this class has both non-native and native English speakers made me feel less nervous about my writing because I know that we are all here to learn English and . . . it is acceptable to make mistakes. It has been a pleasure being in a class that has both native English speakers as well as non-native English speakers as it gave me a sense of belonging and it helped me feel less anxious around native English speakers." (MA, EAP, 2016)

○ "Although enhanced writing skills is not all I gained from taking this course, I have also gained new ways of thinking due to the culturally diverse learning environment W131 provides." (JE, WP, 2018)

From the EAP students' retrospectives, we extracted 22 paragraphs in which they reported gaining cultural understanding. We found 12 such paragraphs in the WP students' essays. The excerpts provided illustrate how the class helped students learn about their own and others' cultures. One student's comment revealed the joy of sharing about one's culture and his appreciation of his peers' interest in learning about it:

○ "I thoroughly enjoyed explaining the Indian culture and festivals to my peers while also understanding the American celebrations like Thanksgiving. I was amazed to see the inquisitiveness of my peers at understanding how other cultures work." (VA, EAP, 2016)

Many comments specified that the diversity of the student population in the class and the approach that pushed them to think from different perspectives led to increased open-mindedness and an improved ability to communicate across cultures.

- ○ "Being in a mixed class allowed us to discuss the different views that each student's background impacted in the perspective of a certain topic, enabling us to accept and understand diverse viewpoints, making us better prepared to deal with differences." (YA, EAP, 2016)
- ○ "I accepted different point of views with a much more open heart. . . . This class helps me express myself in ways I have never thought I could express myself in this multicultural setting." (SI, EAP, 2018)
- ○ "Since I come from a very small town, we do not have a diverse community. . . . I now can write a paper with more of an open mind about the different people who may be reading my paper." (LA, WP, 2018)

Students reflected on how the course affected their language learning or their perception and knowledge of language and writing conventions. In the EAP students' essays, we found 14 such comments, and in the WP students' there were 13, as in these examples:

- ○ "Peer review and interaction with my peers exposed me to several small yet significant writing practices or rules . . . Most of my peers have also been very encouraging and supportive of my work. . . . This class was definitely one of the best and most conducive environments for growth. . . . Taking the writing course with both native and non-native English speakers was a good blend of cultural diversity and served as a great way of overcoming the hesitation I had when approaching native English speakers. This class also assured me that a non-native English speaker can become equally competent in the English language." (VA, EAP, 2016)

○ "Taking an English class that had both non-native speakers and native speakers had a huge impact with my writing. I learned more writing styles from different cultures." (CA, WP, 2016)

○ "The class had an impact on my writing because I got to help the [non-native English speakers] become more accustomed with the English language and writing . . . which also caused me to reflect back on my writing." (ER, WP, 2016)

Both EAP and WP students attributed their writing improvement to the diversity encountered in our internationalized course. In their retrospective essays, students revealed how increased confidence and their exposure to new ideas contributed to their growth as writers.

End-of-Semester Surveys

The 24 EAP students (77 percent of the total) who completed the end-of-the-semester survey were from nine different countries: India (11), Malaysia (5), Vietnam (2), Myanmar (1), Brazil (1), Nigeria (1), Saudi Arabia (1), Israel (1), and Venezuela (1). Twenty-five WP students completed the survey, which was anonymous and was distributed after all other assignments had been collected. Thus, the survey findings are the students' final impression of the Internationalized Writing course experience. The quantitative and anonymous nature of this instrument added more precision and reliability to some findings from the qualitative analysis, as well as new information that was not revealed by the other data sources.

A new piece of information was that most students failed to notice the multicultural, internationalized nature of the course upon enrolling, despite the note we had added into the schedule of classes to single out the class. Fifteen (61 percent) of the 24 EAP respondents enrolled in the course by chance; twelve (48 percent) of the respondents indicated that the class had fit their schedule and that's why they had selected it. The WP students had the same main reasons for enrolling in the class: chance (19 students, 76 percent) and timing (12 students, 48 percent).

The majority of both EAP and WP students, 20 (83 percent) and 23 (92 percent) respectively, revealed that their writing improved significantly in the course. This finding is similar to but more nuanced than statements made in the retrospective essays; in the retrospectives, there was no expectation to specify on a scale how significant one's improvement was, and the students were prompted to provide evidence of how their writing improved. Similarly, for the majority of WP and EAP students—20 (94 percent) and 22 (88 percent) respectively—the main element that made the course effective was the teacher. Occasional compliments to the teacher were made in the retrospective essays as well, but the quantitative survey captured the students' perception more clearly and systematically. In addition, the majority of the EAP respondents—22 (96 percent)—said they would recommend the Internationalized Writing course to others.

When asked how the course was better than other writing courses taken in the past, the few EAP students who had a point of comparison (9, or 39 percent) named several reasons, including that the class gave them a chance to learn about different cultures (2), that it was interactive (2) and challenging (2), and it was not literature-based (1). Two WP students thought the class was better thanks to its diversity.

The survey results show that the course supported cultural development. Slightly more than half of the EAP respondents (12, or 52 percent) thought they significantly improved or improved their cultural understanding and attributed this development to interacting with students from other backgrounds in the class, having to understand their perspectives, and reading their papers. Eleven (44 percent) of the WP respondents also indicated that their knowledge of other cultures improved or significantly improved.

The EAP and the WP students reported similar strengths and challenges as writers; some of these were slightly more pronounced in the EAP group. Most EAP and WP students indicated seldom or never having difficulty with the writing process, engaging in discussion, or communicating with the teacher. About half of the EAP students indicated still having a difficult time incorporating sources, and about one-quarter of them reported difficulties with organization, thesis writing, and grammar. About one-third of the WP students reported the same difficulties, including challenges with grammatical accuracy. Almost all the students found the class activities useful or very useful.

Discussion

Our findings reveal that students valued the Internationalized Writing course because they perceived that it helped them develop as writers and cross-cultural communicators while improving their understanding of culture, language, and writing norms. When we probed the students' impression of their learning before mid-term (in the 2018 and the 2019 peer review responses), we were pleased to learn that they were already becoming aware of the effects of the course well before having an opportunity to reflect on it extensively in their final portfolio retrospective. As is fairly typical, the students were not initially attracted to the course because it was multicultural or internationalized, but they soon valued those elements (Ene & Liu, 2003; Shuck & Wilber, 2018). Our findings imply that programs and institutions should provide opportunities in the curriculum for students to have internationalized learning experiences in FYW because they appreciate them once exposed (as also shown by Saenkhum & Soblo, this volume, and Gherwash, this volume). A higher baseline level of readiness for an internationalized experience, which FYW can provide, may lead to even higher levels of achievement in cultural understanding and writing later in students' academic and professional lives.

As far as the distinctive pedagogical features of the Internationalized Writing course—cross-cultural interaction throughout discussions and stages of the writing process; dialogic activities and assignments designed to raise cultural awareness and trigger reflections on the benefits of participating in such a course; and the topic selection—our findings suggest that these features are important components of the internationalized experience. With regard to interaction and assignments, as hypothesized, the autobiographical narrative laid the groundwork for building community and connecting the students to their own and others' perspectives, providing a portal into deeper exploration and more comfortable cross-cultural interactions throughout the course. The revised peer review responses and retrospectives provided opportunities to reflect, as well as evidence of the course's success. Reflection as a tool for active learning is paramount to gaining a higher level of awareness about what is being learned (Williams, Woolliams, & Spiro, 2012). Therefore, we encourage course instructors and designers to build such features into their internationalized courses and require reflective elements, which can also serve to document the usefulness of the course for institutional and scholarly research.

We found that increased cultural awareness does not happen unprompted, and students benefit from having their attention channeled in specific directions. Not only did we create copious opportunities for intercultural interaction; in peer review responses and retrospective reflections, we intentionally prompted the students to reflect on the effects of the intercultural interaction and focus of the class on their views and writing. To achieve deeper learning, Martins and Van Horn (2018) also suggest shifting "the focus of peer review away from process" to allow students to establish more "meaningful exchanges" (p. 165).

It has been argued since the earliest iterations of cross-cultural/ multicultural composition (Silva, 1994) that a teacher trained in writing and ESL instruction is a crucial component of such a course. Multilingual students in particular value having a trained L2 writing instructor (Shuck & Wilber, 2018, p. 177), as recommended in the *CCCC Position Statement on Second Language Writing and Multilingual Writers* (CCCC, 2020). We take the overwhelming acknowledgment of success from students in this study as a by-product of the teacher's ability to effectively support all students not only as writers but also as language learners and cultural beings. As revealed by our findings, the EAP students were somewhat more preoccupied with their linguistic performance. A number of their comments reflected on the course's success in instilling greater confidence in their writing and facilitating new ways of conceptualizing accents and accuracy. Furthermore, several comments explicitly related student success to the teacher's skill and approach. In her own assessment, Cohen notes that, due to her training and experience in ESL instruction, she is aware of what to expect from students, how to focus on language for both EAP and WP students, and how to guide all students to consider topics from multiple cultural perspectives. Indeed, our WP students also testified that they had to think about others' and their own language in new and deeper ways as a result of the course. Overall, it mattered that Cohen, as teacher of our internationalized FYW course, had expertise in ESL. In addition, Ene's ability to mentor and co-design with the instructor because of her role and expertise improved the programmatic collaboration, the design of the course, and the mentoring of the instructor. The success of Internationalized Writing depends on ensuring that the instructors have the training, mentorship, and programmatic support needed to succeed.

Concerns about teaching WP and EAP students together often stem from the view that the two groups have fundamental linguistic differences and needs (Silva, 1994). This study found that, as writers, the students reported having the same type of challenges and that they were only slightly more pronounced among the EAP students. Unlike in other studies (Mina & Cimasko, 2020; Shuck & Wilber, 2018), the EAP students overcame the discomfort of interacting with WP students. Overall, we are encouraged by the fact that both EAP and WP students reported improving both their writing skills and cultural understanding.

Concluding Thoughts

Internationalized FYW courses offer multiple benefits to students, whether English is their first or additional language: deeper cultural knowledge and understanding; increased confidence in the EAP students' ability to communicate in speech and writing; exposure to some topics not typically addressed in one's culture and, as a result, experience with new or unfamiliar perspectives; and increased awareness of self and others. As a writing course, Internationalized Writing aims to improve students' writing skills. According to our students, this was accomplished in our course. Based on the outcomes of the three iterations of our internationalized FYW course, we recommend it as a model that can be adapted by other programs.

Pedagogically, we agree that the overarching goals for Internationalized Writing should explicitly link writing and cultural learning goals. Courses should "highlight the social and cultural processes in writing" and reflect student awareness of how "social, linguistic, cultural, and national influences" shape their thinking and writing (Martins & Van Horn, 2018, p. 152). Based on this initial study, we see a way to further internationalize our course by explicitly targeting cultural learning by requiring students to:

◯ respond to readings that have an international/global focus

◯ define and reflect on their own culture(s)

◯ analyze and reflect on the connections between culture and perspectives, including their own

◯ reflect on language varieties and audience considerations.

The collaboration between EAP and WP specialists proved fruitful in our case, and we join others in recommending that program and university administrators should work together on curriculum internationalization, building on the strengths of each program to create innovative writing curricula (Gherwash, this volume; Martin & Van Horn, 2018; Saenkhum & Soblo, this volume; Weiser & Rose, 2018).

In our own context and others, FYW course goals could be revisited at the programmatic level to incorporate the cultural understanding goals that guide the EAP curriculum in line with the larger institutionally outlined dimensions of global learning. IUPUI's goals entail enabling "all IUPUI students to have at least one substantial global learning experience during his or her IUPUI career, either internationally or locally" and creating opportunities for students to "analyze their own beliefs, values, assumptions, experiences, and/or communication styles in respect to those of at least one other culture" (IUPUI, 2020, para. 2). In this, our campus is representative of other higher education institutions in the United States. The goal of increasing cultural awareness and understanding, which is integral to achieving internationalization (at home), is articulated in the VALUE Rubrics of the Association of

American Colleges and Universities for both Global Learning (AAC&U, 2014) and Intercultural Knowledge and Competence (AAC&U, 2009), which emphasize "global self-awareness, perspective taking, understanding cultural diversity" and "cultural self-awareness, knowledge of other cultural frameworks, empathy for other cultural groups, understanding of cultural verbal and non-verbal communication, and attitudes of curiosity and openness toward other cultures," respectively. It is more important than ever to make it possible for all students to have a global learning experience at home, given the limited access to study abroad and the importance of intercultural competence in life and workplaces today. As we write this chapter amid the COVID-19 pandemic, we are even more aware of the importance of internationalizing *at home*, through our curriculum. We see FYW as an ideal site for such efforts and for offering all students a global learning experience in collaboration with EAP programs.

REFERENCES

Association of American Colleges and Universities (AAC&U). (2009). *Intercultural Knowledge and Competence VALUE Rubric.* Retrieved from aacu.org

Association of American Colleges and Universities (AAC&U). (2014). *Global Learning VALUE Rubric.* Retrieved from aacu.org

Andrade, M.S. (2006). International students in English-speaking universities: Adjustment factors. *Journal of Research in International Education, 5*(2), 131–154. https://doi.org/10.1177/1475240906065589

Canagarajah, S. (2016). Translingual writing and teacher development in composition. *College English, 78*(3), 265–273.

Conference on College Composition & Communication. (2020). CCC position statement: CCC statement on second language writing and multilingual writers. Retrieved from https://cccc.ncte.org/cccc/resources/positions/secondlangwriting?fbclid=IwAR2 DceB7WSh-NnaD6VUFadx47gTnt8YqzvMbflk1ehKrFlsAwGi0kEphnlc

Crowther, P., Joris, M., Otten, M., Nilsson, B., Teekens, H., & Wächter, B. (2001). *Internationalisation at home: A position paper.* Amsterdam: European Association for International Education.

Ene, E., & Burrup, J. (2001, February 28). Designing cross-cultural composition courses. [Conference presentation]. TESOL conference, St. Louis, MO, USA.

Ene, E., & Liu, J. (2003). *Multicultural composition courses: A viable placement option.* Unpublished manuscript.

Gale: A Cengage Company. (2020). *Gale in context: Opposing viewpoints.* Retrieved from https://www.gale.com/c/in-context-opposing-viewpoints

IUPUI Office of International Affairs: Curriculum Internationalization. (2020). IUPUI dimensions of global learning: Developing global mindsets for all IUPUI students. Retrieved from https://international.iupui.edu/global-learning/curriculum-interna tionalization/global-dimensions.html

IUPUI School of Liberal Arts Department of English. (2018). W131: Reading, writing, & inquiry. Retrieved from https://liberalarts.iupui.edu/english/pages/writing-program -folder/courses.php

Knight, J. (2006). *Internationalization of higher education: New directions, new challenges.* Paris: IAU.

Leask, B. (2009). Using formal and informal curricula to improve interactions between home and international students. *Journal of Studies in International Education, 13*(2), 205–221. https://doi.org/10.1177/1028315308329786

Liu, J. (2001). *Asian students' classroom communication patterns in U.S. universities: An emic perspective.* Westport, CT: Ablex Publishing.

Martins, D. S. & Van Horn, S. (2018). "I am no longer sure this serves our students well": Redesigning FYW to prepare students for transnational literacy. In S. K. Rose & I. Weiser (Eds.), *The internationalization of U.S. writing programs* (pp. 151–169). Louisville: University Press of Colorado/Utah State University Press. doi: 7330/978160732 6762.c008

Matsuda, P. K. (2010). The myth of linguistic homogeneity in U.S. college composition. In B. Horner, M. Lu, & P. K. Matsuda (Eds.), *Cross language relations in composition* (pp. 81–96). Carbondale: Southern Illinois University Press. https://doi. org/10.2307/25472180

Matsuda, P. K., & Silva, T. (1999). Cross-cultural composition: Mediated integration of US and international students. *Composition Studies, 27*(1), 15–30.

Matsuda, P. K., & Silva, T. (2011). Cross-cultural composition: Mediated integration of U.S. and international students. In P. K. Matsuda, M. Cox, J. Jordan, & C. Ortmeier-Hooper (Eds.), *Second-language writing in the composition classroom: A critical sourcebook* (pp. 252–265). Boston: Bedford/St. Martin's.

Miles, L. (2018). Infusing multilingual writers: A heuristic for moving forward. In S. K. Rose & I. Weiser (Eds.), *The internationalization of U.S. writing programs* (pp. 257–272). Louisville: University Press of Colorado/Utah State University Press. doi: 7330/9781607326762.c008

Mina, L. & Cimasko, T. (2020). Expectations, mismatches, and translingual dispositions in teaching multilingual students. In A. Frost, J. Kiernan, & S.B. Malley (Eds.), *Translingual dispositions: Globalized approaches to the teaching of writing* (pp. 63–80). Louisville: University Press of Colorado. doi: 10.37514/INT-B.2020.0438.2.03

Ramage, J. D, Bean, J. C, & Johnson, J. (2006). *The Allyn & Bacon guide to writing.* Custom ed., 4th ed. New York: Longman.

Rose, S.K. & Weiser, I. (Eds.). (2018). *The internationalization of U.S. writing programs.* Louisville: University Press of Colorado/Utah State University Press. doi: 10.7330/9781607326762.c000

Saenkhum, T. (2016). *Decisions, agency, and advising: Key issues in the placement of multilingual writers into first-year composition courses.* Logan: Utah State University Press. http://dx.doi.org/10.7330/9781607325482

Shuck, G., & Wilber, D. (2018). "Holding the language in my hand": A multilingual lens on curricular design. In S.K. Rose & I. Weiser (Eds.), *The internationalization of U.S. writing programs* (pp.168–184). Louisville: University Press of Colorado/Utah State University Press. http://dx.doi.org/10.2307/j.ctt22h6qmq.12

Siczek, M., & Shapiro, S. (2014). Developing writing-intensive courses for a globalized curriculum through WAC-TESOL collaborations. In T.M. Zawacki & M. Cox (Eds.), *WAC and second language writers: Research towards linguistically and culturally inclusive programs and practices* (pp. 329–346). Perspectives on Writing. Fort Collins, CO: The WAC Clearinghouse/ and Parlor Press. http://dx.doi.org/10.37514/PER-B.2014.0551.2.13

Silva, T. (1994). An examination of Writing Program administrators' options for the placement of ESL students in first year writing classes. *Writing Program Administration, 18,* 37–43.

Weiser, I., & Rose, S. K. (2018). Internationalized writing programs in the twenty-first-century United States: Implications and opportunities. In S. K. Rose & I. Weiser (Eds.), *The internationalization of U.S. writing programs* (pp.1–10). Louisville: University Press of Colorado/Utah State University Press. doi: 10.7330/9781607326762.c000

Williams, K, Woolliams, M., and Spiro, J. (2012). *Reflective writing.* Basingstoke, England: Palgrave Macmillan. http://dx.doi.org/10.1007/978-0-230-37724-0

Yam, S. (2018). Interrogating the "Deep Story": Storytelling and narratives in the rhetoric classroom. *Composition Forum, 40.* Retrieved from http://www.compositionforum.com/issue/40/

8

Reaching across the Aisle: Internationalization through Cross-Cultural Composition Courses

Ghada Gherwash

> If the wariness about discomfort is stronger than the desire to hear different viewpoints because engaging difference is uncomfortable, then the quest for diversity is hollow no matter what the demographic statistics on a campus reflect.
>
> —Liebowitz, 2007, para. 23

Small liberal arts colleges (SLACs) can be an optimal environment for achieving internationalization at home (IaH) because of the type of students they attract, but this potential has yet to catch up with their values. Historically, students who gravitate toward liberal arts colleges are "more likely than students at other types of institutions to study abroad and to have international interests" (Green & Siaya, 2005, p. 1). However, SLACs still seem to struggle with internationalization. A 2005 report used six internationalization dimensions (articulated commitment, academic offerings, organizational infrastructure, external funding, institutional investment in faculty, and international students and student programs) to gauge the degree of internationalization at 187 liberal arts colleges. These 187 responses were part of a larger pool of responses to an institutional survey by the American Council on Education entitled "Mapping Internationalization on U.S. Campuses." The report found that about 45 percent of the participating colleges received a medium score in the "international students and student programs" category, and 49 percent scored low. None scored high. Even those who were considered "highly active" in their internationalization efforts did not provide intentional programs to promote internationalization on their campuses. Instead, 63 percent provided students with only "a meeting place . . . to discuss international topics." In contrast, 71 percent of surveyed colleges actively supported structured study abroad programs (Green & Siaya, 2005, p. ii).

These findings seem to suggest that: (1) liberal arts institutions continue to value the study abroad experience more than the diversity on their campuses, and (2) they see the presence of international and domestic students on their campuses as sufficient to promote cross-cultural dialogue. Internationalization research shows that "bringing students from a variety of cultures to study together on an 'internationalization' campus may not be enough to promote the development of intercultural competence for most students" (Lantz-Deaton, 2017, p. 533). Therefore, liberal arts colleges, like other higher education institutions in the United States, need to capitalize on the presence of international students on their campuses by designing programs and courses that will help internationalize their campuses. In this context, internationalization "includes the policies and practices undertaken by academic systems and institutions—and even individuals—to cope with the global academic environment" (Altbach & Knight, 2007, p. 290). On the institutional level, such internationalization efforts could be accomplished through designing programs and courses that aim to foster intercultural communication among students from diverse backgrounds.

Globalization has resulted in an increase in student mobility, where international student enrollment at U.S. institutions reached an all-time high between 2014–2015 and 2015–2016 (Rose & Weiser, 2018, p. 4). Unfortunately, the November 2020 *Open Doors* report on international educational exchange reports a decline of 2.9 percent of international undergraduate enrollment at U.S. institutions (Open Doors 2020). Despite this drop, some U.S. institutions have been able to maintain the number of international students on their campus to those prior to the decline. Colby College, a private SLAC in central Maine with approximately 2,000 students, is a good example of an institution that has retained its enrollment stability and one that has responded positively to small-scale internationalization efforts.

During the national increase in international student enrollment, the number of international students at Colby College has almost doubled over the span of two years. From 2012–2014, it rose to 13.5 percent (Sheriff & Harrington, 2018, p. 116). Since then, international student enrollment has remained steady at around 10 percent. The Office of Institutional Research at Colby, however, only includes F-1 visa students in this figure. To get a clearer picture of how multilingual/multicultural the campus is, when other multilingual groups such as permanent residents and dual citizens are included, the percentage jumps to about 20 percent. The term *multilingual writers* is used to encompass "international visa holders, refugees, permanent residents, and undocumented immigrants, as well as naturalized and native-born citizens of the United States and Canada" who might have grown up speaking languages other than English or non-dominant varieties of English (CCCC, 2020, para. 3). Subgroups of this category will be mentioned when discussing placement procedures.

With the increase in international enrollment at Colby came the need for institutional support structures that would ensure their academic success. When I joined Colby as the inaugural full-time multilingual writing specialist (in 2016), I immediately saw that multilingual writers needed more placement options to increase their agency (Saenkhum, 2016). More specifically, they needed a wider array of writing courses to choose from—more than just mainstream or sheltered, international-only courses. Since mainstream writing classes are the default offerings of writing programs, I developed a course sequence designed to integrate international and domestic students to foster cross-cultural dialogue. This three-course sequence ranged from an international-only course to a cross-cultural first-year writing (FYW) course.

This chapter discusses the unique design and successful implementation of the cross-cultural FYW course (for examples from other types of institutions, see Ene & Cohen, this volume, and Saenkhum &

Soblo, this volume). This chapter includes a brief description of the writing curriculum at Colby, highlighting the importance of collaborative efforts between writing programs and larger administrative support structures within an institution during the placement process, and concludes with snapshots from student reflections that show how the course continues to surpass its initial goals.

Institutional Context and Writing Curriculum

In 2012, Colby hired its first director for the Colby Writing Program (CWP), whose duties included expanding the college's Writing across the Curriculum (WAC) initiative, which started in 2009–2010, and providing pedagogical writing support to faculty across campus. The CWP director had to not only build a program but also develop pedagogical and structural changes within the CWP that would raise faculty's awareness about multilingual pedagogy. Early on, the CWP identified a need for institutional and pedagogical changes that would allow Colby faculty to think "internationally about creating an environment . . . more supportive of linguistic and cultural diversity, and less reflexively monolingual and U.S.-centric" (Sheriff & Harrington, 2018, p. 117). While working with faculty and writing tutors on ways to support multilingual writers, the CWP initiated a labor-intensive, guided self-placement process for all incoming international students. This involves the CWP faculty, in collaboration with relevant stakeholders, reviewing each student's application packet holistically, identifying students who might need additional writing support, and presenting them and their advisors with appropriate placement options. Since guided self-placement does not require a student to take the recommended course, the CWP had to find additional ways to support international students who choose to disregard the recommendation and take a FYW course in their first semester. In 2014, a part-time multilingual writing specialist was hired to provide one-on-one tutorials for multilingual writers; unfortunately, this proved insufficient to meet the increasing demand, so, in 2016, I joined Colby as the first full-time multilingual writing specialist.

In many institutions, the role of a multilingual writing specialist is limited to tutoring and providing one-on-one support for multilingual students. Although this is one of my roles, I am also a writing program administrator (WPA) with faculty title. The intersectionality of my position allows me to participate in curricular conversations and propose changes as needed. When I joined Colby, I quickly identified a need for additional writing courses for multilingual writers and sought to capitalize on the fact that Colby does not use standardized test scores (TOEFL® or IELTS®) for placement. Therefore, the guided self-placement approach seemed ideal for increasing international students' agency during the placement process (Saenkhum, 2016; Silva, 1997). Similarly, Tardy and Whittig (2017) have argued for a "need to design placement processes that effectively support students in selecting from the appropriate options while giving them agency in those decisions" (p. 924). Although Colby had a flexible process, it lacked sufficient options for students to exercise their agency by "negotiating" the options presented to them (Saenkhum, 2016, p. 38; see Ene & Cohen, this volume; Saenkhum & Soblo, this volume).

Colby's WAC model presented students with a menu of FYW classes, but none of these courses was designed with multilingual writers in mind. Thus, students were limited to a pre-FYW course (WP111) they could take if they wished to get their writing "up to speed" so to speak. However, because WP111 is credit/no-credit and does not count toward graduation requirements, some international students did not see the benefit of taking a non-required, pre-FYW course when they could just check off the FYW requirement. Additionally, WP111 was only offered in the fall semester, meaning that if the course schedule did not align with students' courses, they had no alternative courses to support them. Thus, adding credit-bearing courses as additional placement options was crucial to bolster the support the CWP provides, as well as to promote student agency. Silva (1997) argued that "it is necessary to offer [multilingual] writers with as many placement options as possible. According to their abilities and preferences, they should be given the choice of enrolling in *mainstream* composition classes, *basic writing* classes, sheltered [multilingual] classes, or classes designed to *accommodate both native and nonnative speakers of English*" (p. 360; emphasis added). Since Colby offers plenty of mainstream FYW courses, my goal has been to expand on these offerings by designing courses that range from multilingual-only to cross-cultural.

As a start, I built on the WP111 course that Colby already had in place by creating an optional sequence of three writing courses offered throughout the year: fall, Jan-Plan (a month-long semester offered in January), and spring. Students can opt to take all three in any order or opt for only one of them. The fall semester course redesigned WP111 from a writing workshop to a theme-based communications course focused on linguistic and cultural diversity in the United States. The Jan-Plan course (a new course), WP291, was created as an intensive writing course that introduces students to various genres (e.g., rhetorical analysis, reading responses). The third course became a cross-cultural FYW course, the only one in the sequence that fulfills the first-year writing requirement. Because it engages students with global issues, it also satisfies the college-wide "international diversity" requirement and is grounded in the research by Matsuda and Silva (1999), who maintain that an ideal composition course for international students is a cross-cultural one that enrolls both international and domestic students and goes beyond the two-option model of mainstreaming or segregation of multilingual writers. My goals when designing the cross-cultural class were: (1) to draw students' attention to cross-cultural issues of our increasingly internationalized world; (2) to create cross-cultural dialogue and build students' intercultural competence; and (3) to provide more writing course options for multilingual writers.

Course Design

The scholarship in second language writing, intercultural pedagogy, and conversations with colleagues was considered in course design. Although I had been considering the idea of teaching a cross-cultural course, it took a conversation with my colleague Hadi Banat to inspire development of the course (see Banat's forthcoming work with his colleagues in Panahi et al., forthcoming) on transnational curriculum design for writing programs).

I designed the course following the recommendations made by Matsuda and Silva (1999) after they piloted a similar course at Purdue University in 1997, where international and domestic students, in consultation with their advisors, enrolled in the class (see also Reichelt & Silva, 1995). At the time, orchestrating such a placement task through advisors proved to be unsustainable at an institution as large as Purdue University. Colby's size and the composition of its students, on the other hand, seemed to be ideal for such undertaking (see Ene & Cohen in this volume for more on internationalized FYW at a university setting).

Conceptually, I designed the course with Pratt's "contact zones" (1991) in mind. *Contact zones* are "social spaces where cultures meet, clash, and grapple with each other, often in contexts of highly asymmetrical relations of power, such as colonialism, slavery, or other aftermaths as they are lived out in many parts of the world today" (p. 34). Additionally, Amy Lee and her colleagues' framework on teaching interculturally led me to consider my pedagogical choices for the course during the "iterative process for designing, implementing, and continually refining a pedagogy that supports diverse students and intercultural outcomes" (Lee et al., p. 10). Reading their work enabled me to articulate some of the tensions inherent in topical cross-cultural courses; especially relevant to my course design was Solheim's reminder that "intercultural learning is an ongoing process of engagement" (2017, p. 80). She illustrates this point by sharing five tensions she sees as being present in any cross-cultural course (see Table 8.1).

For example, the struggle between the desire to achieve "cultural competence and confidence" and the need to practice "cultural humility" is an ongoing process that involves constant reflection and recalibration. These tensions push students and instructors to think beyond simplistic cultural dichotomies when discussing cross-cultural issues. This framework demonstrates to students the need to rethink cultural competency, showing them that it cannot be fully achieved simply by

TABLE 8.1: Solheim's (2017) Five Tensions

Tension between ...		
Content mastery—knowing about culturally diverse societies	and	Process—knowing how to learn about and interact with culturally diverse societies
Cultural simplicity—knowing that individuals from a particular culture/society behave in an expected pattern	and	Cultural variation—understanding that there is considerable variation within cultures due to intersections with other social locations, such as race, class, gender, etc.
Cultural stability—assuming cultures remain static over time	and	Cultural dynamism—understanding that cultures change and adapt over time
Considering differences of "others"	and	Considering differences of "another"
Cultural competence and confidence—"I have mastered facts about cultural attributes so therefore I know"	and	Cultural humility—knowing what you don't know and being open to ongoing learning through interaction

Reprinted from Teaching Interculturally: A Framework for Integrating Disciplinary Knowledge and Intercultural Development by Amy Lee with Robert K. Poch, Mary Katherine O'Brien, and Catherine Solheim (Sterling, VA: Stylus Publishing, LLC) with permission of the publisher, copyright © 2017, Stylus Publishing, LLC.

taking a few classes that deal with issues of diversity, multilingualism, etc. A cross-cultural FYW course provides an ideal environment for students to start thinking about such issues within an academic setting. In addition to being a great gateway to prime students to think about diversity early on in their college careers, FYW courses can be designed to help students reflect on complex issues through writing.

To further student engagement with the course theme, I assign readings by authors from diverse backgrounds such as Amy Tan, Ha Jin, and Chimamanda Ngozi Adichie. The majority of the course readings are by writers who either speak English as an additional language or speak a non-dominant variety of English. I want students to read first-hand accounts *from* immigrants rather than reading second-hand accounts *about* them. I want students to struggle through some multilingual texts that include more than one linguistic code. These pedagogical choices allow me to use the diversity within the class to empower students to see multilingualism as a resource rather than "a deficit and an obstacle" (Shapiro et al., 2016, p. 31).

Placement and Course Selection

In addition to its international students, Colby has a healthy percentage of generation 1.5 and dual-citizen students who come from linguistically and culturally diverse backgrounds. Colby also has students who are U.S. citizens but grew up outside the United States using language(s) other than English as their primary mode of communication. This type of "hidden diversity" becomes both a challenge and a great educational lesson for stakeholders and students when designing a cross-cultural section.

Because it is challenging to identify multilingual students who are not visa holders for enrollment purposes (Bitchener & Ferris, 2012; Ferris, 1999), I work with the registrar to create a diverse enrollment, aiming for a class evenly split between international and domestic students. It is worth noting here that this process has been problematic because it relies solely on students' immigration/legal status. When working with stakeholders on campus to achieve the desired enrollment for the class, however, I use discussions about the different multilingual groups to raise awareness about the nuanced needs of each of these sub-groups.

What this means in practice is that when registering for classes, Colby students rank their top four alternate choices for a FYW course and then the registrar enrolls them in their top desired FYW course with an open seat. During this process, and before students' schedules are solidified, I work with the registrar to try to balance the enrollment to attain a cross-cultural class.

Course Structure

Writing through the Multicultural Lens is a four-credit FYW course that uses the theme of multiculturalism/multilingualism as a framework to analyze non-fiction texts by writers from various cultural/linguistic backgrounds. More specifically, it focuses on multilingual and multicultural issues (e.g., language and identity, gender stereotypes and changing gender roles, and cultural stereotypes). Its primary goal is to engage students in interrogating and challenging stereotypes about groups/societies/communities that have been prevalent in the news and social media and, in the process, foster cross-cultural communication. The course description explicitly welcomes students who are bilingual/bicultural and those who are interested in issues related to diversity.

Course Units

The course is divided into five units that deal with different aspects of multiculturalism, ranging from accents and linguistic profiling to gender and cultural stereotypes. For example, the first unit, language and identity in personal narrative, presents first-person accounts from bilingual/bicultural writers such as Amy Tan and Dinaw Mengestu. Both share how their experiences with languages and cultures have shaped their identities and their sense of belonging. These readings act as a springboard to help students reflect on their own journeys with literacy/literacies as they prepare for their first assignment, the literacy narrative.

Writing Assignments

In this course, students complete a literacy narrative, a semester-long, four-part research-based project (a proposal, an annotated bibliography, an interview report, and a remediation project) and a capstone portfolio in which they compile and, in a cover letter, reflect on their writing and thinking throughout the semester. The literacy narrative assignment serves two purposes: (1) it enables me to get to know more about each student's experience with literacy across languages, and (2) it gives each student the opportunity to share their own story with literacy within the sociocultural context of their upbringing. The diverse linguistic and cultural backgrounds in the class allow for rich discussions about different educational, linguistic, and familial systems the students might not otherwise have a chance to discuss in depth.

The second assignment is a semester-long research-based project where students work on a topic of their choosing that fits under the major course themes (identity, gender, globalization, stereotypes, etc.) and situate that topic in a country other than their own. Some students choose to write on a topic they are familiar with and try to investigate it within a new country, but the majority choose completely new topics. Some first-generation U.S.-born students who are English-only speakers typically choose to do their research on countries that their parents are from. A few students pick their research based on how little they know about a given country. For example, one student wanted to situate her work in Costa Rica. During the proposal drafting process, when I asked her why she chose Costa Rica, she said, "I pulled up a world map and thought 'What country do I know the least about?' And that's why I chose it." These examples show how this project encourages students to consciously engage with international issues based on familial, educational, or personal reasons.

This semester-long research project also helps cement the relationship the students develop as peer reviewers of each other's literacy narratives, where they get to know more about their peers. Their peer readers could be potential interviewees for the interview report assignment that comes later in the course. Throughout this research project, students work with different institutional support structures, which include a course librarian and a writing fellow, to enhance student learning and complete this four-part project (see section on Institutional Support Structures).

Another assignment that helps students reflect on their intercultural competence is their portfolio, where they compile their work and write a cover letter to reflect on their growth as writers and critical thinkers in relation to the cross-cultural topics of the course. These letters reveal the positive impact this class has had on the way students think about the world around them.

Peer Review Groups

Early on in the semester, students are placed into peer review groups of three to four students, all from different backgrounds. With few exceptions, these groups remain intact throughout the semester because I believe in building a "community of writers" (Elbow & Belanoff, 1999) to allow students to give and receive feedback from classmates, who, throughout the course, become familiar with their strengths and weaknesses as writers. Having diverse members—usually two international and two domestic students—and a task to complete allows students to engage in a cross-cultural dialogue that focuses on discussing and learning about the country and the topic their peers choose to write about. Often times, one member of the peer feedback group happens to be from the country another student in the class is writing about, and in these instances, I observe some of the most interesting cross-cultural conversations in the class between international and domestic students. What makes these conversations valuable is the level of comfort they provide to both parties involved: They are comforting to the student who is exploring a new context to have the opportunity to speak to someone who could provide them with first-hand knowledge, and they also make the international and domestic students' experiences relevant to their peers' learning.

Institutional Support Structures

To achieve its goals, the course makes use of the different student support programs already in place at Colby—the embedded librarian model of instruction and the Writing Fellows Program.

Embedded Librarian Model

The embedded librarian model "emphasizes the importance of forming a strong working relationship between the librarian and a group or team of people who need the librarian's information expertise" (Shumaker, 2012, p. 4). This model of instruction started at Colby in 2018.

I work collaboratively with a librarian throughout the semester who provides students with consistent assistance throughout their research. This librarian co-teaches a unit on academic research with me and also teaches sessions independently on data science and library research, citation software, etc. To tailor her knowledge to each students' needs, she also participates in peer review sessions where students workshop potential topics for their semester-long project. She also holds office hours to assist students outside of class.

Writing Fellows Program

The Farnham Writers' Center (FWC) offers a program that assigns trained tutors to specific courses, upon the faculty's request, to work with students on writing-related aspects of the class as determined by the professor. It emphasizes the importance of drafting and feedback, especially "peer feedback for revision" (Haring-Smith, 1992, p. 124; see also Severino & Knight, 2007; Severino & Traschel, 2008). For this class, the writing fellow attends peer review sessions, holds office hours, and meets with me frequently throughout the semester to discuss students' progress and share any challenges students may be facing with the assignments and/or other course materials. Before the semester begins, we work together to plan her office hours around assignment due dates. To maximize our availability to students, she holds her office hours after business hours, usually 6 pm–8 pm, when most students work on their papers at the library, where the FWC is conveniently located.

Student Reflections

This course has attracted students from different multilingual groups as well as some domestic, monolingual students. Even though the courses use students' legal status as an enrollment criteria, it is not until they start writing their literacy narratives that I truly learn about their unique linguistic and cultural experiences. The structure of the class and its focus allows the students to share personal experiences they might not share otherwise. This is especially true for generation 1.5 and permanent resident students, who might have spent a good portion of their educational lives trying to blend in to avoid the harrowing "ESL" label. Domestic students who identify as monolingual tend to approach this class with caution and are usually the minority in the class. Given the theme of the course, they are usually concerned about the fit for them. These students often express doubt that their presence adds value to conversations about diversity when compared to students who were born outside the United States. I assure them that there is more to diversity than being multilingual and focus the course discussions around the ways that linguistic registers and the different communities they belong to are another way of thinking about multiculturalism. Thus, it is important to create a classroom environment where students feel comfortable sharing what might be labeled as "different" from the dominant culture.

Over time, I have noticed that students in this class interact in ways that make it seem like the rules of the dominant culture do not matter within the classroom space, given that the structure of the course and the diversity among the students does not privilege one group's views over another. Instead, students engage in cross-cultural dialogues where their judgment of difference is suspended. During these interactions, students are more likely to take an introspective stance toward their own views after engaging with multiple perspectives that differ from theirs. For example, instead of using their own culture as a yardstick to judge other students' cultures, the diverse composition of the course leads students to discuss differences as something to be celebrated rather than judged. Creating an environment where diverse ideas are shared allows students to avoid the "us vs. them" dichotomy that often dominates diversity conversations. The impact of these interactions on the students and how they see themselves in relation to the topics discussed is something they write about in their portfolio cover letters, where they are asked to reflect on their growth as citizens and critical thinkers

To show how students perceive and interact with the course topics, snapshots from student reflections are included below. With the exception of one excerpt from an international student that shows how the class has broadened her knowledge about diversity in the United States, I will focus primarily on the experiences of domestic—both multilingual and monolingual—students. However, it is beyond the scope of this chapter to share students' reflections on their growth as writers.

Students' reflections show deep engagement and rumination, exemplifying the three core values of intercultural pedagogy highlighted by Lee et al. (2017), where intercultural pedagogy allows us to "[pursue] equity and inclusion in [the classroom]" and "[recognize] that expertise is fluid and developmental," and helps us "[rely] on and [foster] reflection and revision" (pp. 21–25). The intentional design of a cross-cultural class allows for inclusion and equity among students, creating a space where discussions about "diversity are proactive, rather than reactive or transactional in matters of diversity and equity" (p. 22). Cross-cultural discussions demonstrate to students that learning about diversity and situating themselves within it is an ongoing endeavor—something that cannot be fully accomplished by taking one class. Throughout this process, it is crucial for students to self-reflect on what they know, access what they have learned, and have the courage to admit their gaps in knowledge. The three values of intercultural pedagogy are interwoven throughout students' responses because the course structure is conducive to inclusion and self-reflections vis-à-vis the variety of global issues that are discussed.

For example, one international student expressed her comfort about being in a class with fellow international students where they can easily relate to one another's linguistic and cultural experiences in the United States. Classroom interactions and discussions with domestic students made her aware of the diversity within the United States and how diversity and exposure to different ideas might influence one's identity and concept of self. She noted:

> I think the fact that the class has a lot of international students was really fun; I remember the first reading discussion class when we discussed languages. That was the first time I knew there were bilingual American students in our class, and a lot of them shared multiple identities. I think it would be great if we could introduce our multiple identities at the beginning of class. To be specific, I would like to hear more from the American students. Maybe American students can recognize other American students who may have more than one identity, but these identities are not always clear to international students. Hearing others' experiences from different cultural backgrounds, we learned about other cultures and gained different perspectives. However, I still think we

are very different, because I will only identify myself as Asian, and don't have the sharing feelings of having multiple identities nor the feeling of belonging to America.

This sentiment connects to a domestic-multilingual student's response about how much she enjoyed hearing the diverse voices and opinions in the class and how the constant engagement with her diverse peers pushed her out of her comfort zone. She wrote:

> The classroom discussions, readings, and the semester-long research project all gave me opportunities to ask important questions about multiculturalism. I was fascinated and challenged by the diversity of opinions in our little class. Often a reading that I had loved was hated by another student and vice versa. These moments of disagreement made for interesting conversations and also gave me a window to the unique life experience of my peers. I appreciated the willingness of my classmates to support their opinions by sharing stories of their own experience with the topics we were discussing.

Being able to listen to different perspectives allowed another domestic student to realize how the U.S.-centric education he had received provided him with a one-sided view of the world. He elaborated:

> Because of this class, I have become noticeably more attuned to differences in perspectives. What I found most significant about this class from our readings and discussions was that many of the problems that I originally thought were exclusive to the U.S. were actually global issues. I quickly realized that this was largely due to the education that I have received prior to entering Colby, as it mainly looked at social problems through an American lens. Once I learned to shed this perspective and see the world more holistically, I saw that many other countries not only share similar issues to those of the U.S. but have ones that are vastly different as well. What contributed most to the development of this new perspective were the interactions I was able to have with the many international students who comprised most of the class.

Another domestic student echoed this by sharing her own experience as someone who didn't have much exposure to different perspectives, let alone cultures:

> I received an education which focused mainly on American history and ideals. It almost created a vacuum around me which left me ignorant to many other cultures. With the use of the readings and research that I have partaken in this semester, I have realized the importance of looking at every situation through other lenses besides my own. By looking at things from someone else's point of view, seeing it through the eyes of other people who may be impacted, it allows a better understanding of not only the issue but my fellow citizens. I truly believe that this course has allowed me to be more compassionate, understanding, and open to other cultures and ideas, which will be beneficial to me throughout my life. In the current sociopolitical climate in our world, I believe the values and sense of knowledge which I have gained from this course will allow me to be a better friend and supporter of everyone around me, especially those of different backgrounds.

One of the most powerful of all the reflections I have received was written by a domestic, monolingual student who contemplated dropping the class earlier in the semester, thinking she would not be able to contribute to the diversity discussion. In her own words:

> I was colorblind. Race is something I never feel completely comfortable to talk about out of fear of offending someone by misusing words in unintentional ways or not being politically correct. I was afraid to talk in the first half of the semester, but in turn developed a very acute ear for the stories and lessons that my classmates would tell. I would even argue that listening has changed me as a person more than reading ever will. In class, I love to listen to everyone's point of view on the readings or a given topic, because I find I am much less cultured or opinionated on the topics because I don't experience many racial disadvantages many of my classmates have experienced. And it is eye opening to hear what they have to say,

and even in conversations I rather not participate in, I learn so much more about people, culture, and diversity . . . colorblindness for me was adequate for a while, because I thought it made me a good person. It wasn't until I opened my eyes in this class to see my wrongdoings to my approach to race was I able to appreciate the value of difference. This course has made me more perceptive, aware, and comfortable talking about racial topics, which I would have never felt comfortable openly talking about before.

Her profound growth as a reflective thinker—and listener—made me reassess my previous misconception about students' silence as equivalent to lack of engagement with the course materials. It made me rethink participation grades and how I assigned them in future classes.

Discussion

Matsuda and Silva (1999) held that the development of a successful cross-cultural composition course is contingent upon two factors: "staffing and the placement procedure" (p. 27). This has certainly been the case at Colby College during my time as the multilingual writing specialist. My expertise and training in L2 writing have provided me with the knowledge needed to teach this class, and being a WPA who provides students with recommendations about their placement options also enables me to communicate to the students and their advisors the specifics of the course and its goals. Based on my experience, I would add that it is crucial to get stakeholders to buy into the importance of cross-cultural communication within the institution. At Colby, different stakeholders, such as the registrar, admissions office, and the international office, made it possible for me to have an open dialogue with them about the importance of developing our students' ability to communicate cross-culturally. Their support and the support of the director of the writing program continue to make my class a viable writing course option for international students.

Like many higher education institutions, Colby students are presented with many opportunities to study abroad, but the Colby community seems to take for granted the diversity we have at "home." As described, even though my intent when building the course was to integrate multilingual students into the Colby community, after teaching it for several years, I realize its impact on domestic students has exceeded my expectations. It has become a platform for international *and* domestic students alike to engage in cross-cultural dialogue on an equal footing. Both the course structure and the topics we examine undermine the "asymmetrical distribution of power" (Pratt, 1991, p. 34) between majority and minority groups in the class, empowering all students to share their perspectives.

Concluding Thoughts

Given the newness of the position, it is important that we multilingual writing specialists share our experiences with others who are doing comparable work at similar institutions. Prior to designing the cross-cultural FYW course at Colby, I took a few steps that facilitated my efforts at internationalizing the campus through this course and other initiatives. Bearing in mind that these might not work for other institutions, programs, or settings, I present to program administrators and course designers several steps that worked in my case. First, take stock of the courses that are being offered for multilingual writers and think about them in a way that will provide students with a coherent, sequential learning experience. Second, identify out-of-class support structures for multilingual writers that are already in place and think of ways to use them to enhance student learning in your classes. The campus writing center and the library services are great places to start. As discussed, such support structures have been crucial to the success of my cross-cultural class and to the visibility of the work I do on campus. Third, use the opportunity when proposing a new course or putting forth a new initiative to inform stakeholders about the unique needs of multilingual writers. Complicating common misconceptions about the one-size-fits-all solutions to multilingual writers' challenges should be high on the agenda. Finally, when talking to stakeholders, highlight the importance of internationalizing our campuses from within.

REFERENCES

Altbach, P. G., & Knight, J. (2007). The internationalization of higher education: Motivations and realities. *Journal of Studies in International Education, 11* (3–4), 290–305. https://doi.org/10.1177/1028315307303542

Bitchner, J. & Ferris, D. (2012). *Written corrective feedback in second language writing.* New York: Routledge.

College Composition and Communication (2020). *CCC Statement on second language writing and multilingual writers.* https://cccc.ncte.org/cccc/resources/positions/secondlangwriting

Elbow, P., Belanoff, P. (1999). *A Community of writers: A workshop course in writing.* Boston: McGraw-Hill.

Ferris, D. (1999). One size does not fit all: Response and revision issues for immigrant student writers. In L. Harklau, K. M. Losey, & M. Siegal (Eds.), *Generation 1.5 meets college composition: Issues in the teaching of writing to U.S.-educated learners of ESL* (pp. 98–107). New York: Lawrence Erlbaum Associates.

Green, M. & Siaya, L. (2005). *Measuring internationalization at liberal arts colleges.* American Council on Education. https://www.acenet.edu/Documents/Measuring-LiberalArts.pdf

Haring-Smith, T. (1992). Changing students' attitudes: Writing Fellows program. In S. McKeod, & M. Soven (Eds.). *Writing across the curriculum: A guide to developing programs* (pp.175–188). Newbury Park, CA: Sage.

Lantz-Deaton, C. (2017). Internationalisation and the development of students' intercultural competence. *Teaching in Higher Education, 22,* 532–550. https://doi.org/10.1080/13562517.2016.1273209

Lee, A. Poch, R., O'Brien, M. K., & Solheim, C. (2017). *Teaching interculturally: A Framework for integrating disciplinary knowledge and intercultural development.* Sterling, VA: Stylus.

Leibowitz, R. D. (2007, May 26). The value of discomfort: Baccalaureate address to the class of 2007. Middlebury College. Retrieved from http://www.middlebury.edu/about/president/past/ronald-liebowitz/addresses/archive/baccalaureate2007

Matsuda, P. & Silva, T. (1999). Cross-cultural composition: Mediated integration of US and international students. *Composition Studies, 27*(1), 15–30.

Open Doors (2020). International students in the United States: 2020 fast facts. Retrieved from https://opendoorsdata.org/fast_facts/fast-facts-2020/

Panahi, P., Banat, H., Sims, R., Tran, P., & Dilger, B. (Forthcoming). Transnational curriculum design for intercultural learning in writing programs. In C. Donahue & B. Horner (Eds.), *Teaching and Studying Transnational Composition*. MLA Volume.

Pratt, M. (1991). Arts of the Contact Zone. *Profession*, 33–40. Retrieved from http://www.jstor.org/stable/25595469

Reichelt, M. & Silva, T. (1995). Cross-cultural composition. *TESOL Journal, 5*(2), 16–19.

Rose, S.K. & Weiser, I. (Eds.). (2018). *The internationalization of U.S. writing programs*. Louisville: University Press of Colorado/Utah State University Press. doi: 10.7330/9781607326762.c000

Saenkhum, T. (2016). *Decisions, agency, and advising: Key issues in the placement of multilingual writers into first-year composition courses*. Logan: Utah State University Press.

Severino, C. & Knight, (2007). Exploring writing center pedagogy: Writing fellows programs as ambassadors for the Writing Center. In W. J. MacCauley, Jr., & N. Mauriello (Eds.), *Marginal words, marginal work? Tutoring the academy in the work of writing centers* (pp. 19–34). Creeskill, NJ: Hampton Press.

Severino, C., & Traschel, M. (2008). Theories of specialized discourses and writing fellows programs [Special issue on Writing Fellows]. *Across the Disciplines*, 5. Retrieved from https://wac.colostate.edu/docs/atd/fellows/severino.pdf

Shapiro, S., Cox, M., Shuck, G., & Simnitt, E. (2016). Teaching agency: From appreciating linguistic diversity to empowering student writers. *Composition Studies, 44*(1), 31–52.

Sheriff, S. & Harrington, P. (2018). It's not a course, it's a culture: Supporting international students' writing at a small liberal arts college. In S. K. Rose & I. Weiser (Eds.), *The internationalization of U.S. writing programs* (pp.116–131). Louisville: University Press of Colorado/Utah State University Press. doi: 7330/9781607326762.c008

Shumaker, D. (2012). *Embedded librarian: Innovative strategies for taking knowledge where it's needed*. [eBook edition]. Information Today Inc. https://ebookcentral.proquest.com

Silva, T. (1997). On the ethical treatment of ESL writers. *TESOL Quarterly, 31*(2), 359–363. https://doi.org/10.2307/3588052

Solheim, C. (2017). Case study. In A. Lee, A. R. Poch, M. K. O'Brien, & C. Solheim (Eds.), *Teaching interculturally: A framework for integrating disciplinary knowledge and intercultural development* (pp. 77–98). Sterling, VA: Stylus.

Tardy, C. M., & Whittig, E. (2017). On the ethical treatment of EAL writers: An update. *TESOL Quarterly, 51*(4), 920–930. http://www.jstor.org/stable/44984798

9

Guided Writing Instruction Groups: Connecting L2 Graduate Writing Proficiency to Academic Culture and Language

Lucie Moussu and Silvia Sgaramella

Writing is a social act that graduate students need to perform to develop research literacies and build their identities as scholars (Badenhorst & Guerin, 2015); they do this by finding "a voice that resonates with the academic community" (Ondrusek, 2012, p. 179). Lack of adequate writing instruction, however, can slow this process. Graduate students spend much of their careers being novices, partly because they are not formally taught about the writing expectations and genres required at their level of studies (Strasser, 2007). These students, whether writing in their first (L1) or second/additional (L2) language, face the same demands (Huang, 2013), in that both groups of students are expected to master "academese," or academic/research writing, without clear guidance. For those writing in an L2, this demand is further complicated by possible culture shock and adjustments to new academic contexts. In addition, the assumption that L2 graduate students need to focus primarily on their language skills (Jones et al., 1995) devalues the importance of their writing process.

Fortunately, academese "can be actively taught" (Badenhorst & Guerin, 2015, p. 16). For example, Huang (2013) suggested the use of workshops focusing on metacognition to gain genre awareness, while at the same time keeping individuals' needs in mind based on their linguistic backgrounds (p. 26). Huang's strategy can be particularly helpful in developing the scholarly potential of L1 and L2 graduate students and can, in turn, promote conversations among students and scholars. These conversations foster internationalization at home (IaH), defined here as a cluster of activities to add an "international dimension" to the practices in higher education, excluding domestic student mobility (Nilsson, 2003, p. 31).

This chapter describes a pilot study investigating the application of a new model called Guided Writing Instruction Group (GWIG). Developed by the director of the writing center (WC) at a large Canadian university, with the help of two graduate tutors, this model was first offered in January 2016. This non-traditional model evolved from the more traditional writing group pedagogy merged with a non-credit course model. The goal of GWIGs is to facilitate the acquisition of academic writing conventions among L2 graduate students, and to respond to frequent requests for writing help by these students, their departments, and their supervisors. Additionally, GWIGs help boost students' self-confidence and improve their communicative skills so that they can become active members of their discourse communities.

This chapter provides a theoretical and pedagogical framework for GWIGs, describes this model in detail, shares the results of a small pilot study, discusses the implications for university practices, and provides suggestions for future research on the topic of IaH.

Issues and Challenges That Motivated the Research

Our GWIG model is founded on four conceptual pillars: Vygotsky's sociocultural theory, writing group pedagogy, socioliterate approaches to writing, and non-credit pedagogy. Vygotsky (1984) argued that the process of cooperation and social communication is crucial for the higher mental functions of the child (e.g., speech). When it comes to teaching writing, the social constructivist notion of collaborative learning supports the adoption of peer response to foster the linguistic development and writing skills improvement of both L1 and L2 speakers of English (Ferris & Hedgcock, 2005). Similarly, collaborative learning and social interaction in L2 acquisition, especially in the form of group work, strongly contribute to language development (Ferris & Hedgcock, 2005). In turn, collaborative learning helps L2 students improve their linguistic proficiency while socializing with their local academic community (Brooks-Gillies, Garcia, & Manthey, 2020) and, therefore, helps develop their scholarly identities in a foreign environment.

The contemporary concept of the writing group (or circle) and its pedagogy originated from a social constructionist approach to teaching writing by "draw[ing] on the social aspects of peer learning [and] linking the development of research literacies with emerging academic identities" (Lee & Boud, 2003, as cited in Badenhorst & Guerin, 2015, p. 18). The term *writing group* was adopted by Gere (1987) to clarify the ambiguity surrounding what was becoming a widely used pedagogy. Gere identified as irrelevant the high number of terms employed to define this phenomenon (e.g., helping circles, collaborative writing, writing laboratories, teacherless writing, group inquiry technique, editing sessions, mutual improvement sessions). All of these terms indicate a group of writers providing peer feedback on one another's work, independently from format or academic affiliation. Aitchison and Guerin (2014) provided a similar definition when applying this type of pedagogy to graduate studies.

While writing groups may be offered in multiple formats (Badenhorst & Guerin, 2015; Gere, 1987; Haas, 2014), one trait that they all share is their foundation in writing as a social practice (Gere, 1987). This social function can also be shared in the L2 context. Indeed, when it comes to L2 writing, Silva (1990) proposed that writing groups should be considered "purposeful and contextualized communicative interaction, which involves both the construction and transmission of knowledge" (p. 18). Writing thus becomes a foundation for achieving the research literacies that will shape L2 students' scholarly identities. According to Street (1995), the use of the term *literacies* is also an indicator of the social nature of literacy itself, as it underlines "the multiple character of literacy practices" (p. 2). In fact, the notion of Literacy with a capital *L* and ending with a *y* (p. 2) has been replaced in academic writing by "discipline-specific rhetorical forms" and the idea that multiple audiences hold different expectations based on field (Ferris & Hedgcock, 2005, p. 13). In other words, literacy events are writing activities among peers who share specific conventions generated through their interactions. Through these events, peers participate in literacy practices that then generate literacy approaches shared by their community (Ferris & Hedgcock, 2005; Riazi, 1997). These approaches, also named *genre pedagogy* (Badenhorst & Guerin, 2015), are grounded in both the multiple character of literacies—as a product of reading, writing, and speaking—and their placement within a sociocultural context (Ferris & Hedgcock, 2005). Such approaches are relevant to L2 writers because they need to cultivate an awareness of the writing conventions (both linguistic and rhetorical) of specific genres and fields of research (Ferris & Hedgcock, 2005; Cooley & Lewkowicz, 1997; Swales & Feak, 2012). These approaches also allow L2 writers to learn about "knowledge, learning . . ., and themselves" (Ondrusek, 2012, p. 180). It can then be inferred that Badenhorst and Guerin's (2015) support of genre pedagogy was grounded in the necessity to equip L2 students with the tools they need to succeed as researchers and scholars.

Finally, our GWIG model also stems from non-credit pedagogy, a type of informal curriculum that includes non-assessed support services and learning activities offered by a university alongside the formal, credit-bearing curriculum (Leask, 2015). When students are not pressured to produce for good grades, they are allowed to learn at their own pace, and learning outcomes in the non-credit system are not measured by grades but by the ability to apply learned skills to specific environments (Keech, 2013). For the GWIG model, students demonstrate learning by using the strategies and experience they have acquired in writing group meetings. Indeed, Badenhorst and Guerin (2015) affirmed that students (especially L2 students) often feel anxious and inadequate when they write about their research. Non-credit pedagogy also seems useful to the acquisition of linguistic and rhetorical skills, as the language-learning process is a very personal, recursive, and unpredictable journey through trial and error. Also, when tests and grades are not a concern, the learning process can become the focus. Keech (2013) described this aspect as part of the process of becoming "citizens"; such reasoning can be extended to academia, where graduate students are required to become citizens of their local scholarly communities. This process can also be related to the notion of "being local" based on their own personal experience (Selasi, 2014); students can become "local" through their graduate school experience in a specific discourse community, while at the same time their experience in other realities enriches that community and contributes to IaH. In fact, when L2 graduate students become an integral part of their new local reality, they can participate in scholarly activities, such as conferences and publications. This "multilocality" facilitates the exchange of ideas with domestic students and scholars, providing different perspectives.

We deliberately adopted this knowledge-exchange pedagogy in our GWIGs to facilitate appropriate language use, rhetorical moves, and long-term knowledge retention, allowing student writers to progress from a "knowledge-transforming" stage of development (i.e., transforming knowledge for the benefit of the writer) to a "knowledge-crafting" stage (i.e., communicating knowledge to a reader) (Kellogg, 2008, p. 3).

Local Context and Characteristics of the Model

Based on the pedagogical principles just described, our GWIGs focus on the needs of both our institution (i.e., a large research university) and our L2 graduate students. On the one hand, GWIGs combine characteristics common to many institutional non-credit writing-related resources offered to graduate students (e.g., writing groups, workshops, courses, bootcamps). Figure 9.1 shows some of these resources.

On the other hand, formal elements of credit courses allow our GWIGs to run efficiently. These elements include a consistent instructor, a flexible but structured syllabus, detailed lesson plans, weekly

FIGURE 9.1: Types of Instruction Contributing to the GWIG Model

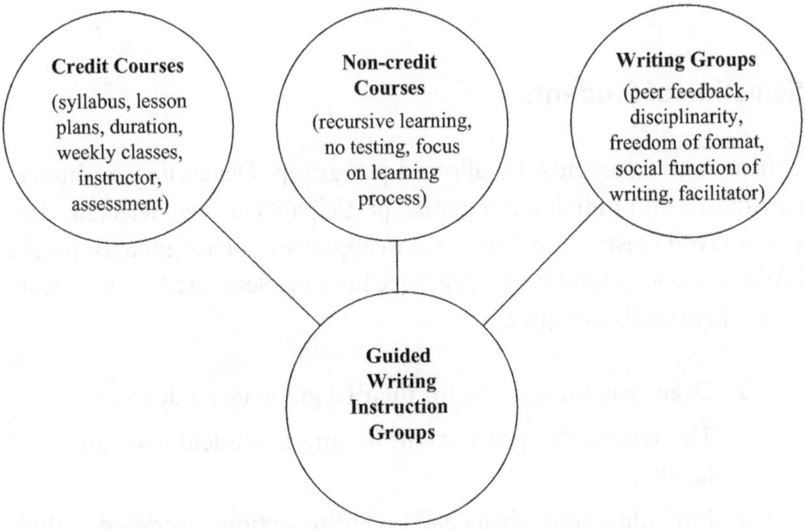

classes, and some self-assessment. They also provide a structure that students and the institution recognize and respond to well.

Consistent Instructors

Weekly class meetings are taught throughout an entire term by the same graduate WC tutor (the instructor), who is responsible for every aspect of the course: selecting participants, designing the syllabus, selecting materials and activities, teaching, and giving feedback. Importantly, GWIG instructors are trained peer writing graduate tutors, which allows them to use one-on-one tutoring practices in class and increases the sense of shared discourse and experience. Instructors, who can be L1 or L2 speakers of English themselves, greatly benefit from leading GWIGs by interacting with and learning from students with diverse linguistic, cultural, and educational backgrounds. In addition, since our instructors study in various faculties (arts, science, education, etc.), the WC director can, for example, assign tutors studying engineering to teach GWIGs restricted to engineering students.

Selection of Students

Ten to twelve students are allowed per group. Depending on budget constraints and individual requests, participants are self-selected, chosen by GWIG instructors from a list of applicants, or assigned to specific GWIGs. Various funding models have been implemented—some more or less logistically complex:

○ Deans pay for sections for their L2 graduate students.

○ The WC funds open sections for any L2 student from any faculty.

○ Individual supervisors pay for entire sections restricted to their own L2 students (e.g., students in one lab).

○ Individual supervisors pay for one or more of their students to attend a GWIG.

○ Individual L2 students ask their dean to fund sections for them.

○ Individual units/departments pay for sections restricted to specific students (e.g., Chinese exchange students, sponsored students).

Although some students offer to self-fund to attend GWIGs, the WC director has always rejected this option, as it would create inequality between students who can afford the GWIG and those who cannot.

Disciplinarity and Interdisciplinarity

Applicants to open sections are selected according to the stage of their studies (e.g., starting their dissertation), not according to disciplines.

Instructors can also select applicants who are working on similar projects (e.g., candidacy paper) or are encountering similar linguistic difficulties. Similarly, if the dean of science funds a GWIG for L2 students in science only, that group can include students from any science department. During the term, participants and instructors become familiar with academic conventions relevant to them, while also learning about their peers' research fields through peer reviews and in-class discussions.

Assessment

Instructors use a writing sample requested before classes start to assess participants' writing skills and the genres with which they engage. During the first class meeting, instructors also administer a writing inventory and a personal goals worksheet, allowing instructors and participants to start reflecting together on their writing practices, field-specific genres, attitudes toward writing, and stylistic preferences. Participants can also set goals for themselves and refer to them throughout the course.

Topics

Many topics are covered during the semester, including pre-writing techniques, active reading, cohesion and coherence, rhetorical grammar, editing techniques, formatting styles, structure of a data commentary, qualifying a claim, sentence variety for rhetorical purposes, organization of a methods section, expressions of limitations, abstracts, discourse communities, audience expectations, and cross-cultural communication. A general list of possible topics is provided by the WC director, and specific topics are discussed and selected by the instructor and the participants based on their specific needs. Although each topic can be taught independently and classes have a workshop format, there is an intentional continuity in the way (and order in which) topics are taught. For example, sentence variety can be taught to build up the foundation for rhetorical grammar.

Flexible Syllabus

Unlike credit courses, this unique model does not have a fixed syllabus. Instead, instructors draft a syllabus based on best practices (scaffolding, etc.), as well as information gained from the writing samples, the writing inventory responses, and the personal goals worksheets. This draft syllabus is then discussed and negotiated with participants to maximize learning and to ensure that students' goals and expectations are met. It can be revised during the course if participants and/or the instructor discover that needs and goals have changed.

Instruction and In-Class Writing

Class meetings are structured in two parts: for one hour, the instructor teaches the topic of the day; then students participate in discussions and activities to practice the topic of the day and/or work on their own projects, applying what they have just learned. For example, to improve students' paraphrasing skills, the instructor could first show the differences between paraphrasing and summarizing and include strategies to address both. Then, students could look at correctly and incorrectly paraphrased texts. Further, the instructor could provide paraphrasing exercises to solidify the concepts. An online platform (e.g., Google Docs) would allow the instructor to see what students are writing and to provide immediate feedback if necessary. During the second part of the class, students could choose to work on their own writing individually or in pairs, applying their new paraphrasing skills, or they may prefer to continue working on extra texts/exercises. Meanwhile, the instructor would circulate to answer questions and provide quick one-on-one feedback on students' work.

Peer Response and Exchange

Peer activities can be used during the second hour of class to discuss one of the participants' pieces of writing, or students can work together on exercises on the topic of the day. Peer exchange can also be used to help participants practice certain grammar rules by, for example, reading each other's drafts and looking for certain types of errors. Students can also practice explaining their choices (transitions, rhetorical moves, etc.) to their classmates. During this time, students are also welcomed to talk about interactions and challenges with their classmates and supervisors in a safe, confidential environment.

Online and Face-to-Face Feedback

Between class meetings, students submit a draft of their writing (two or three pages) to their instructor for individual written feedback, which is then briefly discussed with each student during the second part of the next class meeting, while the other students continue working on their projects or exercises. During this phase, the instructor functions as a WC tutor and applies principles of WC theory and practice, such as prioritizing higher-order concerns, fostering writers' confidence by pointing out the strengths in their writing, and asking targeted questions to lead students to learning.

Research Questions

At the end of 2017, after two years of continuous writing groups, we decided to investigate the impact of these GWIGs on participants' writing skills and analyze their end-of-course feedback. Until then, the model had been well received by the L2 graduate community, graduate tutors, thesis supervisors, and faculty members. In fact, the first time the project ran, three groups were opened (with 10–12 places available in each group) and 252 students applied (Moussu, 2016, p. 80). Nevertheless, we wanted to analyze students' progress and feedback more systematically.

These research questions guided our pilot study:

1. Which writing skills do students possess before attending GWIGs?
2. How do students' writing skills improve when attending GWIGs? In which areas is improvement visible?
3. What do students think about GWIGs?

Research Methods

Data Collection Procedures

After receiving IRB approval, we collected writing samples from GWIG participants at the beginning and end of each term (winter, spring/summer, and fall 2018). Forty-eight students agreed to participate. By year's end, 33 students had submitted both an initial and a final writing sample that we used to answer Questions 1 and 2. In addition, as is the case at the end of every term, all GWIG participants were sent an online feedback form. In 2018, 78 anonymous responses were collected (Moussu, 2018; 2019) and analyzed to answer Question 3.

Data Analysis Procedures

To answer Research Questions 1 and 2, a systematic analysis of participants' writing skills at the beginning and end of each term was conducted. A rubric was created with four categories that were further divided into subcategories. Subcategories within Language and Mechanics were given weights according to their complexity and significance, while subcategories within Content and Organization were calculated as an average of the items (see Table 9.1).

Initial and final drafts were rated using a scale from 1 to 5 according to these ranges:

5–4.1 Excellent

4–3.1 Good

3–2.1 Satisfactory

2–1.1 Minimally Acceptable

1–0 Unsatisfactory

To answer Question 3, student feedback was first coded using categories (e.g., course content, organization of course, student goals and

TABLE 9.1: Weighted Rubric for the Evaluation of Initial and Final Drafts

Category 1. Language		
Item		**Mean**
Register / Tone	Appropriate to genre, audience, and purpose (including jargon, tone, concision, persuasiveness)	20%
Grammar / Syntax / Sentence Structure	Standard and clear word order; correct grammar (i.e., verb tenses, articles, prepositions, subject/verb agreement, pronoun/ antecedent agreement, singular/plural, adverbs/adjectives, modals), sentence boundaries, sentence variety (i.e., simple, complex, compound-complex)	30%
Diction	Precise, correct word choices and usages/forms (i.e., I was boring vs. I was bored)	30%
Voice	Appropriate sense of the writer's presence, perspectives, opinions	10%
Concision	Efficient use of language	10%

Category 2. Content		
Item		**Mean**
Claim(s)	Avoids sweeping / unsupportable claims	33.3%
Research / Sources	Present/not present; selection/appropriateness; handling and management (i.e., quotations/paraphrases present, well-chosen, appropriate length/number, used to support own ideas; not used as independent ideas; sources introduced/contextualized and explicated/ analyzed)	33.3%
Engagement / Idea Development	Thoughtful/deep vs. cursory/surface thinking and application; sufficient, well-chosen, and clear examples, facts, and details; explicit arguments/connections; sufficient/clear explanations; sufficient/ effective analysis	33.3%

Category 3. Organization		
Item		**Mean**
Cohesion (macro)	Logical organization/flow; thesis matches body of text; thesis order followed in entire body; effective topic sentences; effective headings and subheadings	50%
Cohesion	Transitions within paragraphs and within sentences; appropriate recurrence of key words and terms	50%

Category 4. Mechanics		
Item		**Mean**
Use of References	Correct in-text citation; correct Works Cited/References/ Bibliography (e.g., MLA, APA, IEEE)	20%
Spelling	Correct spelling	30%
Punctuation	Correct use of periods, commas, colons, apostrophes, question marks, and other punctuation marks	50%

expectations, instructor preparedness). These categories were then tallied using simple percentages.

Findings and Discussion

Research Questions 1 and 2

When categories were collapsed, participants' initial and final drafts overall scored as indicated in Table 9.2:

When comparing initial-draft ratings with final-draft ratings in each category, students' drafts did not seem to have improved significantly in three of the four categories (Language, Content, and Mechanics). However, they seemed to have improved significantly ($p < .002$) in the Organization category.

Results in the Language sub-category (Table 9.1) show that participants already had a strong understanding of genre. Grammar and diction also did not constitute a significant issue, being assessed as "good," while voice and concision were "satisfactory." These findings seem to debunk the assumption that L2 graduate students primarily need to work on language skills (Jones et al., 1995) to improve their papers and meet expectations.

Unsurprisingly, the Content category (Table 9.1) shows that participants were fully aware of the need to use supporting sources appropriately and avoid unsupportable claims. This reinforces our findings that L2 graduate students are familiar with the genres they are required to

TABLE 9.2: Overall Rating for Participants' Initial and Final Drafts

Overall Rating for Each Category Initial Draft		Overall Rating for Each Category Final Draft	
Language	3.9	Language	4.2
Content	3.8	Content	4.5
Organization	2.8	Organization	3.7
Mechanics	3.9	Mechanics	4.2

use in academic writing. In addition, within the Content category, idea development was satisfactory. This means that, despite participants' familiarity with specific genres, they still needed to work on expressing their thoughts—in particular via use of examples, explanations, and connections to guide their readers. Responses about the writer's voice in the Language category, scored as satisfactory, further support the notion that L2 graduate students need guidance, first to improve their knowledge-crafting skills through writing (Kellogg, 2008) and second to achieve a stronger voice to affirm their academic identity (Aitchison & Lee, 2006; Matsuda, 2015).

In the Mechanics category (Table 9.1), participants scored between good and excellent on spelling and use of references and satisfactory on punctuation; these results also seem to debunk the familiar assumption that students struggle in these areas. In fact, participants' initial writing samples show that, although Language and Mechanics improvements are still necessary, L2 graduate students already have strong language foundations.

Finally, the most significant changes appeared in the Organization category (Table 9.1), where participants' initial drafts were considered "minimally acceptable," while their final drafts were assessed as "good." This finding challenges the notion that writing instruction should primarily focus on language (Ferris, 2004). In fact, our results show that the most substantial issue in these students' writing is cohesion, both between and within paragraphs. This is consistent with the Content category findings when it comes to idea development: students are not fully aware of the organizational conventions regarding academic writing in the the Canadian/US context and, therefore, apply the structures they were taught in their previous academic contexts. Student papers showed a lack of thesis statements, transitions between and within paragraphs, and connections between introductions and conclusions, which are typical of the academic genre in the US and Canada but are not necessarily implemented elsewhere. Such inconsistent structure alongside occasional grammatical and mechanical errors can cause reader/supervisor frustration and may promote the incorrect notion that grammar is the primary issue that needs to be addressed.

Research Question 3

All GWIG participants received a feedback form at the end of the term. The first question asked participants to explain their goals. One student's response summarized the participants' overall feelings quite well: "I took this course so my supervisor doesn't scream at me and destroy my thesis anymore!" The participants' other goals included:

○ wanting to improve their writing skills (51 percent of participants)

○ figuring out their writing weaknesses and learning about grammar, punctuation, structure, concision, etc. (43 percent)

○ developing better writing habits and confidence (21 percent)

○ wanting help to finish their thesis or dissertation (14 percent)

When asked if their goals had been achieved, 76 percent of the participants responded "yes," 22 percent responded "to some extent," and 2 percent responded "a little" or "I'm not sure." When asked what they liked about their GWIGs, students responded that they:

○ appreciated their helpful, patient, well-prepared, and/or encouraging instructor (41 percent)

○ liked the friendly atmosphere of the course (36 percent)

○ loved the weekly feedback from their instructor (28 percent)

○ felt the course increased their confidence (12 percent)

○ enjoyed the multidisciplinarity of the other participants and/ or the assignments (9 percent)

When asked what they disliked about their GWIG, participants answered:

○ "nothing" (61 percent)

○ some of the assignments and/or the way the course topics were organized (19 percent)

○   meetings/course length, because they needed help over a longer period of time (e.g., a full year instead of one term) (11 percent)

○   classmates who were not engaged in the course and/or were annoying and/or asked "stupid questions" (9 percent)

○   the course did not focus on their specific field of study (7 percent)

Finally, when asked if they believed their academic writing skills had improved over the term, 92 percent of the participants said "yes" and 8 percent of the participants answered "partially."

In summary, the answer to Question 3—What do students think about GWIGs?—is that participants were mostly satisfied. They appreciated their instructor's encouraging teaching style and the engaging atmosphere of class meetings, and they were grateful for their instructor's feedback. A few students complained about the organization of the course, but most participants believed they had significantly improved their writing skills. As many as 98 percent of the participants responded that they had fully or to some extent achieved the initial goals they had set when they joined their GWIGs. Only 12 percent of the participants responded that the GWIGs had increased their confidence, but other students' confidence might have improved without them noticing it or remembering to mention it in our open-ended questionnaire.

A significant finding of this pilot study is that students seemed to believe that they needed to improve their grammar skills more than anything else and expected our GWIGs to do just that. In reality, however, grammar skills did not seem to be what L2 graduate students struggled with the most. Instead, students seemed to need to learn about the many aspects of academic writing: rhetorical moves, the strengths and weaknesses of their own writing practices, and, more importantly, their valuable participation in and contribution to the academic conversation (see for example Ondrusek, 2012, for a list of 12 core competencies of advanced writing skills). Cross-cultural awareness, metalinguistic skills, and self-confidence will enable students to have more productive discussions about their writing challenges and about the support they need from their supervisors, as well as the institution, to continue improving their writing skills beyond our GWIGs. Cross-cultural awareness, meta-linguistic skills, and self-confidence will also enable international students to engage fully and equitably in academic conversations so that language is no longer a barrier, and they, together with domestic students, feel that they truly belong to their discourse community.

Implications for Practice and Future Research

A systematic analysis of the pedagogies applied to our GWIG model indicates several benefits for participants and peer instructors. First, given the foundational element of non-credit pedagogy, the lack of testing reduces anxiety by creating a safe space for learning through trial and error. At the same time, our model provides social and emotional support for writers (Williams, 1990) since participants are allowed to discuss their drafts, as well as share their frustrations toward their writing process with a peer instructor who will not judge or grade them. Given a risk-free space to discuss their challenges and fears, time to focus on their writing at their own pace, and supportive feedback, participants are able to create a better final product over the academic term (Lavelle & Bushrow, 2007). In addition, deliberate practice and shared participation in social and communicative activities can lead participants and institutional actors (instructors, supervisors, and other scholars) to not only achieve significant writing goals but also improve academic and personal conversations among peers from different linguistic and educational backgrounds. These conversations are crucial to improve audience awareness, promote idea exchanges, and cultivate a global discourse and perspective in the scholarly community, thereby contributing to IaH.

Another advantage of non-credit pedagogy is that it allows for a better alignment between assessment and instruction through the use of continuous practice and repetition, facilitating learning and long-term retention (Keech, 2013; Kellogg, 2008). The application of this approach to this course model allows topics to be practiced for a longer period of time or expanded further if the instructor and/or the students believe that a concept has not been acquired. For example, students might not fully grasp a new concept like "rhetorical grammar," but this recursive approach will allow instructors to spend more time on the concept than initially planned.

Finally, the focus on learning that characterizes non-credit pedagogy is meant to cultivate awareness of one's own writing process, as well as audience expectations, intercultural competence, rhetorical moves, and writing conventions in different fields of research and different countries. A deeper understanding of the North American academic discourse and its cultural particularities will enable both L2 graduate students and their peer GWIG L1 and L2 instructors to become more sensitive to differences among diverse student populations.

While our GWIG model promises benefits that go beyond those listed here, adjustments are sometimes still required as the model is a work in progress. Some areas to consider involve funding, criteria for participant selection, syllabus and lesson plan design, course materials selection, number and length of meetings per week, and in-class activities. These, as well as student concerns, should be investigated further in the future.

Regarding the implications of our results, we believe our GWIGs proved to be excellent support systems for L2 graduate students to learn about the complexity of academic discourse, while at the same time acquiring domain-specific knowledge (Ondrusek, 2012). Our GWIGs are also great opportunities for domestic peer instructors (or regular instructors, if necessary) to learn from and interact/engage with group participants. These GWIGs are not cheap but are more efficient than one-on-one instruction in WCs or supervisors' offices. In addition to offering language and writing support, GWIGs can help students recognize their actual writing strengths and weaknesses, learn how to communicate effectively about their research and writing choices, start feeling that they belong to the greater academic conversation and community, and acquire the tools necessary to continue improving these skills beyond GWIGs. There are many compelling reasons to suggest that all graduate programs would benefit from providing this kind of teaching and learning support to their L2 graduate students and L1 or L2 GWIG instructors.

Ideally, L2 graduate students' supervisors would familiarize themselves with the findings of this study and others (see Kellogg, 2008; Ondrusek, 2012; Tardy, 2016) to become aware of strategies that enable students to write and communicate more effectively. In the meantime, GWIGs can provide participants with the awareness, knowledge, and tools they need to negotiate and complete their graduate school writing tasks more efficiently. Further, students are not constrained within predetermined boundaries but are exposed to different spaces where transfer and transformation of learning can happen (Larsen-Freeman, 2013). Thus, students can acquire research literacies and be empowered to build their scholarly identities, thereby allowing them to actively participate in their academic discourse communities (Brooks-Gillies, Garcia, & Manthey, 2020). Students are then not merely "socialised into academic contexts and taught how to conform to existing cultures" but rather are "able to 'read' the discourse and then decide if they want to conform, transform or resist" (Badenhorst & Guerin, 2015, p. 15). In other words, our GWIG model should facilitate the formation of L2 graduate students' scholarly identities and develop their awareness of their reading and writing strengths and weaknesses, as well as their confidence.

While our study looked at the improvements seen in participants' writing and communication skills after a term of instruction, we realize that such improvements can take a lifetime (Kellogg, 2008). Therefore, it would also be useful to interview the participants' thesis/dissertation supervisors and the GWIG participants about their long-term feedback. We hope that the present work can motivate other institutions to develop and expand our model further based on individual needs and contexts (e.g., for undergraduate L2 students). This study can also serve as a foundational step to further investigate the linguistic and rhetorical skills and awareness of GWIG participants. Also needing to be investigated are the cross-cultural long-term effects of GWIGs on both instructors and participants, the opinion of participating L1 and L2 speakers, and supervisors' opinions on their students' progress. Such considerations will strengthen GWIGs' role in IaH by providing support and opportunities for L2 graduate students to thrive; in doing so, these students can fully articulate their international perspectives and different mindsets, while feeling equally validated as their L1 peers in their contribution to their respective academic fields. This would also reinforce the notion that L2 graduate students are an asset for any domestic institution and should be valued accordingly.

REFERENCES

Aitchison, C., & Guerin, C. (2014). Writing groups, pedagogy, theory and practice: An introduction. In C. Aitchison & C. Guerin (Eds.), *Writing groups for doctoral education and beyond: Innovations in practice and theory* (pp. 3–17). New York: Routledge, Taylor & Francis.

Aitchison, C., & Lee, A. (2006). Research writing: Problems and pedagogies. *Teaching in Higher Education, 11*, 265–278.

Badenhorst, C., & Guerin, C. (2015). Post/graduate research literacies and writing pedagogies. In C. Badenhorst & C. Guerin (Eds.), *Research literacies and writing pedagogies for masters and doctoral writers* (pp. 3–28). Leiden, Netherlands: Brill.

Brooks-Gillies, M., Garcia, E. G., & Manthey, K. G. (2020). Making do by making space: Multidisciplinary graduate writing groups as spaces alongside programmatic and institutional places. In M. Brooks-Gillies, E. G. Garcia, S. H. Kim, K. Manthey, & T. G. Smith (Eds.), *Graduate Writing Across the Disciplines: Identifying, Teaching, and Supporting* (pp. 191–209). Fort Collins and Louisville, CO: The WAC Clearinghouse; University Press of Colorado. https://doi.org/10.37514/ATD-B.2020.0407.2.08

Cooley, L., & Lewkowicz, J. (1997). Developing awareness of the rhetorical and linguistic conventions of writing a thesis in English: Addressing the needs of EFL/ESL postgraduate students. In A. Duszak (Ed.), *Culture and styles of academic discourse* (pp. 113–129). New York: Mouton de Gruyter.

Ferris, D. (2004). The "Grammar Correction" Debate in L2 Writing: Where are we, and where do we go from here? (And what do we do in the meantime...?). *Journal of Second Language Writing, 13*(1), 49–62. doi:10.1016/j.jslw.2004.04.005

Ferris, D., & Hedgcock, J. (2005). *Teaching L2 composition: Purpose, process, and practice* (2nd ed.). Mahwah, NJ: Lawrence Erlbaum.

Gere, A. R. (1987). *Writing groups: History, theory, and implications.* Carbondale: Southern Illinois University Press.

Haas, S. (2014). Pick-n-Mix: A typology of writers' groups in use. In C. Aitchison & C. Guerin (Eds.), *Writing groups for doctoral education and beyond: Innovations in practice and theory* (pp. 30–48). New York: Routledge, Taylor & Francis.

Huang, L. (2013). Academic English is no one's mother tongue: Graduate and undergraduate students' academic English language-learning needs from students' and instructors' perspectives. *Journal of Perspectives in Applied Academic Practice, 1*(2), 17–29. doi:10.14297/jpaap.v1i2.67

Jones, E. A., Hoffman, S., Moore, L. L., Ratcliff, G., Tibetts, S., & Click, B. A. L. (1995). *National assessment of college student learning: Identifying college graduates' essential skills in writing, speech and listening, and critical thinking.* Washington, DC: Office of Educational Research and Improvement, U.S. Department of Education. (ERIC Document Reproduction Service No. ED383255).

Keech, G. (2013, May 1). *What is noncredit?* Retrieved from https://ww2.kqed.org/learning/2013/05/01/what-is-noncredit-2/

Kellogg, R. T. (2008). Training writing skills: A cognitive development perspective. *Journal of Writing Research, 1*(1), 1–26. doi:10.17239/jowr-2008.01.01.1

Larsen Freeman, D. (2013). Transfer of learning transformed. *Language Learning, 63*(1), 107–129. doi:10.1111/j.1467-9922.2012.00740.x

Lavelle, E., & Bushrow, K. (2007). Writing approaches of graduate students. *Educational Psychology, 27*, 807–822.

Leask, B. (2015). *Internationalizing the curriculum.* New York: Routledge.

Lee, A., & Boud, D. (2003). Writing groups, change and academic identity: Research development as local practice. *Studies in Higher Education, 28*(2), 187–200.

Matsuda, P. K. (2015). Identity in written discourse. *Annual Review of Applied Linguistics, 35*, 140–159.

Moussu, L. (2019). *2018/2019 Annual Report.* Retrieved from https://www.ualberta.ca/media-library/ualberta/students/centre-for-writers/documents/final-annual-report-2018-to-2019.pdf

Moussu, L. (2018). *2017/2018 Annual Report.* Retrieved from https://www.ualberta.ca/media-library/ ualberta/students/centre-for-writers/documents/annual-report-2017-2018.pdf

Moussu, L. (2016). *2015/2016 Annual Report.* Retrieved from https://cloudfront.ualberta.ca/-/media/ ualberta/students/centre-for-writers/documents/annual-report-2015-2016.pdf

Nilsson, B. (2003). Internationalisation at home from a Swedish perspective: The case of Malmö. *Journal of Studies in International Education, 7*(1), 27–40. doi:10.1177/1028315302250178

Ondrusek, A. (2012). What the research reveals about graduate students' writing skills: A literature review. *Journal of Education for Library and Information Science, 53*(3), 276–288.

Riazi, A. (1997). Acquiring disciplinary literacy: A social-cognitive analysis of text production and learning among Iranian graduate students of education. *Journal of Second Language Writing, 6*(2), 105–137. doi: 10.1016/S1060-3743(97)90030-8

Selasi, T. (2014). *Don't ask where I'm from, ask where I'm a local.* TEDGlobal 2014, Rio de Janeiro, Brasil. https://www.ted.com/talks/taiye_selasi_don_t_ask_where_i_m _from_ ask_where_i_m_a_local?language=en

Silva, T. (1990). Second language composition instruction: Developments, issues, and directions in ESL. In B. Kroll (Ed.), *Second language writing: Research insights for the classroom* (pp. 11–23). New York: Cambridge University Press.

Strasser, E. (2007). Writing what matters: A student's struggle to bridge the academic/ personal divide. *Young Scholars in Writing, 5*, 146–150.

Street, B. V. (1995). *Social literacies: Critical approaches to literacy in development, ethnography, and education.* London: Longman.

Swales, J., & Feak, C. (2012). *Academic writing for graduate students: Essential tasks and skills* (3rd ed.). Ann Arbor: University of Michigan Press.

Tardy, C. (2016). *Beyond convention: Genre innovation in academic writing.* Ann Arbor: University of Michigan Press.

Vygotsky, L. S. (1984). *Sobraniye sochineniy* [Collected works] (Vols. 1–6). M.G. Yaroshevskiy (Ed.). Moscow: Pedagogika. (Original manuscripts, ca. 1930–1934).

Williams, T. (1990). The gift of writing groups. *The English Journal, 79*(4), 58–60. doi:10.2307/818130

Index

Printed and bound by CPI Group (UK) Ltd, Croydon, CR0 4YY

09/06/2025

14685635-0001